MANCHESTER UNITED

– THE 25 YEAR RECORD

1974-75 to 1998-99

SEASON BY SEASON WRITE-UPS
David Powter

EDITOR
Michael Robinson

CONTENTS

British Library Cataloguing in Publication Data
A catalogue record for this book is available from the British Library
ISBN 1-86223-041-2

Copyright © 1999; SOCCER BOOKS LIMITED   (01472-696226)
72, St. Peters' Avenue, Cleethorpes, N.E. Lincolnshire, DN35 8HU, England

Printed by The Cromwell Press

MANCHESTER UNITED F.C.
Seasons 1974-75 to 1998-99

The 1998-99 campaign ended on an amazingly dramatic and victorious note for Manchester United, when last gasp strikes by substitutes Teddy Sheringham and Ole Gunnar Solskjaer snatched the European Cup from under the noses of Bayern Munich. This formed the third leg of an unprecedented 'Treble' – following successes in the Premiership and F.A. Cup earlier in May. It was a different story, however, 25 seasons before when the club experienced second-flight football for the first time in 37 years, after Tommy Docherty's side had been relegated in 21st place at the end of 1973-74.

United's stay in the Second Division lasted just one term. They won their first four games and never relinquished the lead, finishing three points ahead of Aston Villa. Despite United's relegation there was one Manchester derby in 1974-75, in the League Cup, with Docherty's side winning 1-0. Two more top-flight sides, Burnley and Middlesbrough, also found visits to Old Trafford too hot to handle. However, Norwich City (who had also inflicted United's first League defeat) destroyed United's Wembley hopes in the semi-final.

Manchester United made a magnificent return to the First Division, rattling up five wins in an unbeaten six game run which took them to the top of the early 1975-76 table. Although they were unable to sustain that relentless pace, they remained inside the top five and retained title hopes until Stoke City beat them at home in late April. United eventually had to settle for third place, four points behind Champions Liverpool.

For some weeks, though, the Old Trafford faithful had dreamed of achieving the 'Double', with their team storming to the F.A. Cup final. However, even one trophy proved elusive when under-dogs Southampton beat them 1-0 in a disappointing final.

United fans brushed the cobwebs off their passports for the club's first European campaign in eight years in 1976-77. A 1-0 defeat at Ajax did not deter the Red Devils, who responded by winning the return 2-0. They followed up with a 1-0 home win over Juventus, but then crashed out of the UEFA Cup in Turin.

In the League, Docherty's side made a good start and headed the table after eight games before losing form and going eight games without a win. They failed to get back on terms with the leaders and finished sixth. However, silverware was captured in 1976-77 as United reached their second successive F.A. Cup final and this time beat Liverpool 2-1. Stuart Pearson opened the scoring in the second half, but United conceded an equaliser almost immediately. Yet, within another two minutes, Jimmy Greenhoff deflected home a shot from Lou Macari, to destroy Liverpool's 'Double' dream.

It was Manchester United's first major trophy in nine years, however, it proved to be Docherty's last achievement with them. He lost his job as a result of an affair with the wife of the club's physiotherapist and was replaced by Dave Sexton.

Sexton's side made a good start to 1977-78, but slowly lost form and drifted to lie 14th at Christmas. The signing of the Leeds pair, striker Joe Jordan and centre-half Gordon McQueen, led to some improvement and they finished 10th.

United were involved in an eventful European Cup Winners' Cup campaign in 1977-78. They pulled off a superb 1-1 draw at St. Etienne, but the headlines were grabbed by the exploits of some of their fans who caused disturbances. United were initially thrown out of the competition because of that bad behaviour, but were allowed back on appeal, with the condition that the return leg was played at least 300 kilometres from Old Trafford. It eventually went ahead at Home Park, Plymouth, in front of a 31,500 crowd (with nearly as many watching on closed-circuit TV at Old Trafford). Goals by Stuart Pearson and Steve Coppell ensured United's progression, but Porto proved too good for them in the second round.

There were few highlights in the League in 1978-79 with Sexton's side finishing ninth, winning just twice in their last 13 games. The distraction of an F.A. Cup run was partly to blame as, for the third time in four seasons, they reached the final. The Wembley encounter with Arsenal was no classic, but it did have an explosive twist in its tail. Trailing 2-0 with just four minutes remaining, McQueen and Sammy McIlroy sensationally pulled United level; however, they lost concentration, and the Cup, as the Gunners fired a dramatic late third to avert extra-time.

Sexton recruited his old Chelsea skipper Ray Wilkins during the summer of 1979 and the midfielder's arrival led to greater consistency. United headed the table in October, and from then onwards disputed the lead with Liverpool. However, a 6-0 defeat at Ipswich tipped the balance their rivals' way and, despite a run of eight victories from nine games, United had to settle for the runners-up berth in 1979-80, two points adrift.

The following season's UEFA Cup run was brief and undistinguished, with Widzew Lodz bundling them out on away goals. With Wilkins side-lined until January, United struggled to find their rhythm in the League. Too many games were drawn and, despite losing only once in the first third of the season, they could not keep pace with the leaders. Sexton's £1 million dabble on Garry Birtles was not a success, the former Forest striker failed to score in 25 League appearances. United won their last seven matches of 1980-81 to finish eighth, but it was not enough to prevent Sexton from being sacked and replaced by Ron Atkinson.

The new boss soon rang the changes, bringing in Frank Stapleton to replace the AC Milan-bound Jordan (top scorer for the previous two terms). Atkinson also added John Gidman and then returned to West Brom, his previous club, for Remi Moses and Bryan Robson.

Following a mixed start to 1981-82, United climbed to the top of the table in late autumn, but could not maintain their challenge and finished third. Stapleton top scored with 13, while Birtles contributed 11 goals.

After crashing out of the UEFA Cup to Valencia, United concentrated on the domestic front in 1982-83. The signing of Ipswich's Arnold Muhren proved to be a masterstroke and Atkinson's side lost only once in the first 11 games to head the table towards the end of October. A dip in form coincided with Wilkins' absence with a broken jaw. Wilkins lost the captaincy of both his club and country during this period to Robson, while arguably United lost the chance of taking the title. They won only nine of their last 24 games, but still finished third.

The Champions Liverpool defeated them in the Milk Cup; but only after extra-time in a thrilling Wembley final. Wilkins was back in the side, but Robson was missing through injury. Norman Whiteside gave United the lead, but they could not hold on.

Atkinson's side returned to Wembley two months later for another close and exciting encounter, in the F.A. Cup final with Brighton & Hove Albion. The Seagulls scored first, but United responded with goals from Wilkins and Stapleton. A late equaliser set up extra-time, during which Brighton wasted a golden chance and a relieved Manchester contingent were grateful to return for a replay. This time they made no mistake, with Robson (2), Whiteside and Muhren on the score-sheet in a 4-0 victory.

A fine start of eight wins from the first 11 games set United up for another title challenge in 1983-84. A 16 game unbeaten run kept them in contention; however, they picked up only three points from their final five games and had to be content with fourth place.

A contributing factor in their Championship failure was the distraction of a lengthy Cup Winners' Cup campaign. Dukla Prague, Spartak Varna and Barcelona were all beaten en route to the semi-final with Juventus. However, after being held 1-1 at Old Trafford, United's hopes evaporated in Turin.

The following season United enjoyed another good run in Europe, beating Raba Gyor, PSV Eindhoven and Dundee United before being edged out in a penalty shoot-out by Videoton in the UEFA Cup quarter-final.

Wilkins had by now departed to AC Milan and United's midfield had been supplemented on the flanks by Gordon Strachan and Jesper Olsen. After a muted start of four draws, United moved into the top four. However, they could never get on terms with emphatic Champions Everton and finished fourth.

Manchester United and Everton met four times in 1984-85. The Toffeemen came out on top in the League, winning 5-0 at Goodison Park and grabbing a point at Old Trafford. They also won 2-1 in the Milk Cup; but United had the final word in the F.A. Cup final. It took a replay to by-pass Liverpool in the semi-final and extra-time before they ended Everton's double bid at Wembley. However, Whiteside's fine goal was not the full story as United had Kevin Moran sent-off (making him the first man to walk in an F.A. Cup final) and so their success was even more creditable.

United made a magnificent start to 1985-86, conceding just three goals and scoring 27 times in winning ten games on the trot. They were not beaten until their visit to Hillsborough in early November. However, the rot slowly set in as Robson missed a huge chunk of the remainder of the season through injury. League leadership was finally lost on 1st February as Atkinson's side buckled under pressure. They finished fourth, 12 points adrift of Champions Liverpool.

In stark contrast to a year earlier, 1986-87 opened with three defeats and after nine games United were floundering in the relegation zone with just five points. A short flurry of better results lifted them to 19th; but even so Atkinson was sacked in November. Alex Ferguson was appointed as the new manager and United gradually improved to finish 11th.

The improvement continued in 1987-88 with just two defeats before Christmas and only three more afterwards. However, United never gained the leadership and had to settle for the runners-up berth, nine points behind Liverpool. Close season signings Brian McClair (the top scorer with 24) and Viv Anderson had made a noticeable difference, as did mid-season signing Steve Bruce.

Jim Leighton and Mark Hughes (who rejoined from Barcelona) were the fresh faces at the start of 1988-89. Only one of the first 15 games was lost, but nine ended in draws and Ferguson's side struggled to keep up with the pacemakers. Six wins from seven fixtures after Christmas lifted them to third; but six defeats in the last eight games meant they only finished 11th. United did reach the F.A. Cup quarter-final stage, but exited to Nottingham Forest at Old Trafford.

Manchester United went all the way in the F.A. Cup the following season and gave Ferguson his first trophy as their manager. Oldham Athletic were beaten in a semi-final replay to set up a final meeting with Crystal Palace. A thrilling first game ended 3-3 with Hughes netting twice and Robson getting the other. The more subdued replay deservedly went United's way with full-back Lee Martin the unlikely scorer.

United had a mediocre season in the League in 1989-90 and only a late flurry of wins lifted them to 13th place. Part of the problem was the large influx of new faces, who took time to bed in. Over £2 million was spent on Neil Webb and Mike Phelan during the close season. Then, Gary Pallister, Paul Ince and Danny Wallace made their debuts after big money moves.

There was a marked improvement in consistency in 1990-91 and sixth place was achieved. McClair and Bruce were the joint top scorers with 13, the latter's tally including 7 penalties. A different sort of penalty was the one inflicted on the club for the events in their home defeat by Arsenal. At one stage all 11 United players and the 10 outfield Gunners were involved in a mass brawl. As a result both clubs were fined £50,000, Arsenal were deducted two points and United lost one. On a happier note, Ryan Giggs made his initial appearances on the team-sheet in 1990-91 and scored in the Manchester derby at Old Trafford.

The club reached two cup finals in 1990-91. Firstly, they beat Leeds home and away to reach the Rumbelows Cup final for a meeting with Sheffield Wednesday. United were the favourites, but on the day the Second Division side, managed by Ron Atkinson, deserved their 1-0 triumph.

The second final was the club's first in a European competition since they won the European Cup in 1968. Pesci Munkas, Wrexham, Montpellier and Legia Warsaw were knocked out to set up a meeting in Rotterdam with Barcelona. The final was a tight affair, but a brace by Hughes turned it United's way. The Spanish side fought back and halved the deficit, but it was Bryan Robson who lifted the European Cup Winners' Cup to the great delight of the travelling United fans.

It was another Spanish side, Atletico Madrid, who ended United's hopes of retaining the trophy in 1991-92, at the second round stage. However, there was one major cup success in 1991-92 when United returned to Wembley for another Rumbelows Cup final. This time they were on the right end of a 1-0 score-line, with McClair's goal defeating Nottingham Forest.

The 1991-92 League campaign started in excellent fashion with an unbeaten run of 12 matches. After losing 3-2 at Hillsborough, United went on another fine run which yielded 16 points from six games. The title run-in had turned into a two horse race with Leeds United.

The absence of the injured Robson was a contributory factor to an inconsistent run of just six wins from 16 games, which was punctuated by a glut of draws. Leadership swapped hands several times, but it was Manchester United who held the initiative with a one point lead and a game in hand on the morning of Easter Monday. However, Forest exacted some revenge for their Wembley defeat by winning 2-1 at Old Trafford. Leeds took over again at the top and two days later the game in hand, at West Ham, was frittered away in the second half. Leeds refused to falter and took the title by five points.

Manchester United made an indifferent start to the inaugural Premier League campaign, in 1992-93, and stood as low as 10th in November. The turning point was Ferguson's plunge into the transfer market to sign Eric Cantona from Leeds. That £1.2 million investment was to be repaid handsomely.

Cantona soon ignited his new team-mates and, with a ten game unbeaten run, United moved to the top of the table and another head-to-head battle, this time with Aston Villa. Memories of the previous season flooded back when United hit a four match winless sticky patch around Easter. However, this time, they refused to crack and finished with seven consecutive victories. Villa could not match the pace and finished ten points adrift.

So, after a gap of 26 years, Manchester United were again Champions. Further injuries meant that Robson had only a bit part in the triumph. Cantona had been the catalyst, but this was a great team performance. Peter Schmeichel had been magnificent between the sticks, while Paul Parker, Bruce, Pallister and Dennis Irwin formed a formidable back four.

Ince had been an influential figure, linking defence with attack; and Giggs, Lee Sharpe and Andrei Kanchelskis were the cutting thrusts on the flanks. The unsung McClair switched from attack to midfield to accommodate Cantona, and he and top scorer Hughes (with 15) never gave less than 100% commitment.

Earlier in 1992-93, the club's UEFA Cup campaign was ended at the second round stage by Torpedo Moscow. After two goalless draws, the Russians sank United in a penalty shoot-out.

Ferguson's men also exited at the second round stage of the European Cup a year later when Galatasaray proved to be unexpectedly difficult opponents. The Turks pulled off a major shock by drawing 3-3 at Old Trafford, while the second leg was goalless.

United were left to concentrate on trying to land a unique domestic treble. A six match unbeaten run sent them to the top of the table at the end of August, and they never really looked back despite a 1-0 defeat at Stamford Bridge. They reeled off another 21 games without defeat before Chelsea completed the double over them. The next defeat was more significant as it was against their main rivals Blackburn Rovers, which reduced the gap to just three points (with seven games remaining). However, United kept their nerve and retained the title without playing, when Rovers went down at Coventry. The final points tally was 92 (a club record), eight more than Blackburn. The 1993-94 success was gained by virtually the same personnel as twelve months earlier, with the addition of summer signing Roy Keane.

Dreams of the treble had evaporated when former boss Ron Atkinson out-foxed them in the Coca-Cola Cup final. His Aston Villa side won 3-1 with Andrei Kanchelskis receiving a late red card. His suspension ruled him out of a return to Wembley, two weeks later, for an F.A. Cup semi-final with Oldham. The Latics were generally the better side and took the lead in extra-time; however, with only seconds left Hughes volleyed a spectacular equaliser to set up a Maine Road replay. Kanchelskis returned to spark a convincing 4-1 victory and set up a final with Chelsea.

Ferguson's team became only the fifth side to win the 'Double' when they beat Chelsea 4-0. The first half was goalless; but United then took control, and the F.A. Cup for the eighth time, with Cantona (two penalties), Hughes and McClair netting.

There was no Bryan Robson at Old Trafford the following season. He became Middlesbrough's player-manager after making 345 appearances and scoring 74 goals for United. 1994-95 promised to be another great campaign for Robson's old side, but in the end was cloaked with disappointment. United's participation in the European Cup foundered in December when they finished third in their group. They failed to progress to the knock-out stages after conceding three more goals than Barcelona who, with IFK Göteborg, finished above them.

In a bid to boost his side's fire-power, Alex Ferguson signed Andy Cole from Newcastle for

£7 million. The new striker netted 12 times (including six in the 9-0 thrashing of Ipswich); but could not quite make up for Cantona's loss in the last four months of the season. The Frenchman had been banned following an outrageous attack on a spectator during the match at Crystal Palace in January.

Even without Cantona, United pushed Blackburn all the way to the line, but failed by just one point. With Rovers slipping up at Anfield, Alex Ferguson would have collected his third successive title if his side had won (rather than drawn) at West Ham on the final day. Further disappointment followed in the F.A. Cup final, when Everton defeated them by a single goal.

Having narrowly missed out on both major domestic trophies in 1994-95, United bounced back the following term to clinch their second 'Double' in three campaigns. Paul Ince joined Internazionale (for a club record fee received of £7 million) and Mark Hughes departed for Chelsea (after netting 119 goals in 345 appearances during his two spells at Old Trafford) in the close season. There was no incoming activity on the transfer front, however as the club's youth development programme continued to pay dividends in the shape of Nicky Butt, Paul Scholes, David Beckham and Phil Neville (following in the footsteps of brother Gary). All became regular members of the first-team squad during the course of 1995-96.

A ten match unbeaten run left Ferguson's side well placed behind leaders Newcastle United in the early tables. A pre-Christmas slump, which embraced defeats at Liverpool and Leeds, handed the Magpies a ten point advantage at Christmas. However, the Red Devils immediately got back on track with goals by Keane and Cole defeating the leaders on 27th December.

After that United swept to the title in majestic fashion, dropping only ten points in the second half of the season, to finish four points in front of Kevin Keegan's side (who had held a 12 point lead in January). The 1-0 victory at an otherwise impregnable St James' Park in early March proved decisive. Cantona, notched that key goal and followed up with strikes in the next five crucial fixtures. Although suspension had prevented him making an appearance until October, the Frenchman again finished top scorer, with 14 goals.

United made an unconvincing start to their F.A. Cup campaign, when held at home by Sunderland. In fact, it took a late equaliser by Cantona to keep them in the competition and were again troubled by the First Division side at Roker Park, before coming from behind to win the replay 2-1. After winning at Reading, United were pushed hard by neighbours City at Old Trafford, but overcame them 2-1 with the help of a disputed penalty. The scorers Cantona and Sharpe were also on target at Old Trafford in the quarter-final when Southampton were defeated by two second half strikes. More second period joy followed in a Villa Park semi-final, with goals by Cole and Beckham edging out Chelsea who had led at the break.

The final with Liverpool was a rather disappointing spectacle, brightened only by the spectacular volley from 'Footballer of the Year' Cantona which secured the trophy. The Frenchman became the first foreigner to skipper a side to F.A. Cup glory, ensuring Manchester United clinched an unprecedented double 'Double'.

United's interest in both the UEFA Cup and Coca-Cola Cup evaporated at the first hurdles in 1995-96. Second Division York City took their scalp in the latter competition, while Rotor Volograd knocked them out of Europe despite a dramatic late headed goal by Schmeichel.

Old Trafford became even more cosmopolitan in 1996-97 with the arrival of Norwegians Ronny Johnsen and Ole Gunnar Solskjaer; the Czech Republic's Karel Poborsky, and the Dutchman Jordi Cruyff. Making way were former skipper Steve Bruce (who joined Birmingham City) and Leeds bound Lee Sharpe. Hopes of domestic cup glory evaporated at the fourth round stage of both competitions. Eventual winners Leicester City defeated them in the Coca-Cola Cup, while Wimbledon forced them out of the F.A. Cup in an Old Trafford replay. Manchester United still had ambitions of lifting two trophies deep into the season, though, with a fourth Premiership Crown and a second European Cup clearly in their sights.

Despite losing half their group games (twice to Juventus and also more surprisingly at home to Fenerbahce), United qualified for the knock-out stages of the European Cup. A convincing 4-0 home display effectively took care of Porto in the quarter-final to set up two matches with Borussia Dortmund. The Germans scored late on their home pitch and early at Old Trafford to leave Ferguson's side with too much to do and disappointingly they slipped out 2-0 on aggregate. It was of no consolation that their victors went on to lift the trophy – beating Juventus in the final.

The League campaign started well with a nine match unbeaten run, but three successive defeats checked United's stride. Astonishing 5-0 and 6-3 reverses at Newcastle and Southampton, respectively, were followed by a 2-1 defeat at home to Chelsea. However, despite the distraction of their lengthy European campaign, United went on to lose only two of their remaining 26 fixtures to finish seven points ahead of Newcastle United, Arsenal and Liverpool. Solskjaer was the top scorer with 18 goals – seven more than Cantona who rather surprisingly decided to retire at the season's end. The Frenchman netted 64 goals in 143 appearances in Manchester United colours, winning four League Championship medals and two F.A. Cup winners medals in his glorious five seasons' stay at Old Trafford.

The new face in the United squad for 1997-98 was England striker Teddy Sheringham, a £3.5 million purchase from Spurs. Ferguson's side led the early tables and did not lose until the end of September when Leeds United beat them 1-0. That Elland Road encounter set the Red Devils back far more than three points though, as skipper Keane badly injured himself making a tackle and was to be side-lined for the remainder of the campaign. Nine of the next 11 League games ended in victory, though, as Manchester United made their mark at the top of the table.

Their only other pre-Christmas defeat was at Highbury, but it was the second match with Arsenal in mid-March that really opened up the Championship race. At one stage, earlier in March, United held an 11 point advantage (having played two more games) but the Gunners' single goal victory at Old Trafford took them within six points, with three games in hand. Although United did not lose another game, Arsenal's ten consecutive wins proved enough to clinch the title. Alex Ferguson's side finished as runners-up – one point adrift.

Their European Cup run also ended in ultimate disappointment, despite powering into the last eight after winning their first five group games. Kosice and Feyenoord were defeated comfortably home and away, while Juventus were beaten 3-2 at Old Trafford. The Italian side extracted revenge in the final group game, beating the Red Devils 1-0 to accompany them into the quarter-finals. United were well positioned to reach the last four when they held Monaco to a goalless draw in the first leg; however, they conceded an early goal at Old Trafford and slipped out of the competition on away goals after drawing 1-1.

There were some key changes in personnel at Old Trafford during the summer of 1998. Gary Pallister (who made 317 appearances) joined Middlesbrough and veteran striker Brian McClair (88 goals from 355 appearances) took a coaching role at Motherwell. Joining the club were Jesper Blomqvist and Jaap Stam, the latter costing a club record fee of £10.5 million from PSV Eindhoven. That record was shattered early in the new season, though, when Aston Villa were paid £12.6 million for Dwight Yorke. Another significant change to take place during the campaign was the departure of assistant-manager Brian Kidd, who became Blackburn's manager. His replacement as Fergie's number two was Derby County's first-team coach Steve McClaren.

The new signings greatly strengthened the squad and with Keane back in full flow after his injury, United were a formidable force in 1998-99. Although their Worthington Cup hopes ended at the quarter-final stage, the men from Old Trafford went on to clinch the 'Treble', achieving an unprecedented third 'Double' in the process.

The race for the Millennium's last title went to the wire, with the main challenge coming from Arsenal and Chelsea. Manchester United failed to beat the London pair in the League with the Gunners one of three sides to beat them during the first half of the season. However, despite their prolonged involvement in other competitions, United held their nerve to finish the campaign with an unbeaten 20 match run. With Arsenal still only a point behind them on the final day, Ferguson's side could not afford to slip up in their home game against Spurs. Old Trafford quivered briefly when the visitors took an early lead, but goals by Beckham and Cole ensured that United clinched their fifth title in seven years. Yorke was one of three men to head the Premiership scorers' list with 18 goals. His great friend Cole netted just one less, while the under utilised Solskjaer netted 12 times – including four from the bench in the 8-1 hammering of Nottingham Forest.

Eight games were required to capture the F.A. Cup for the tenth time in the club's history. Late strikes earned home victories over Middlesbrough and Liverpool. After also beating

Fulham at Old Trafford, United eventually edged past Chelsea in a Stamford Bridge replay. A second match was also needed in the semi-final following a goalless encounter with the holders Arsenal. Roy Keane's dismissal in the replay appeared to hand the advantage to the North Londoners. The Gunners missed a great opportunity (even failing from the spot) to take their place in the final and 120 minutes of pulsating football will always be remembered for Ryan Giggs' magnificent dribble and shot to win the tie 19 minutes into extra-time. The final proved to be a routine 2-0 win, with Newcastle United succumbing rather meekly as substitute Sheringham and Scholes got their names on the scoresheet.

The F.A. Cup final was of course not to be the club's final match of the season, that came four days later when Bayern Munich were their opponents in the European Cup final. United reached that stage by side-stepping LKS Lodz in the qualifying round and then progressing from a group which contained Bayern Munich, Barcelona and Brondby. The Red Devils were unbeaten but only managed to defeat the Danish side twice. Both of the Barcelona games incredibly finished 3-3, while the two matches with the Germans also ended all-square.

After defeating Internazionale 2-1 on aggregate, United faced their old foe Juventus at the semi-final stage. A last minute goal by Giggs ensured the home leg ended 1-1 and then United edged a five goal thriller in Turin to reach the European Cup final for the first time in 31 years. After conceding an early goal, United struggled to find their rhythm in front of 90,000 at the Nou Camp and Bayern Munich seemed set to take the trophy. However, there was to be a dramatic finale. With 90 minutes on the clock and Schmeichel desperately pushing forward, Sheringham squeezed home an equaliser. With the Germans still in shock, 102 seconds later, another substitute Solskjaer poked home the close range winner. The European Cup was on its way back to Old Trafford and Alex Ferguson had emulated Sir Matt Busby's achievement in 1968. It was no surprise when Ferguson himself received a Knighthood shortly afterwards.

Lifting the European Cup crowned Peter Schmeichel's eight year stay at Old Trafford, as soon afterwards he moved to Sporting Lisbon. Undoubtedly the great Dane's huge presence will be missed but, with Sir Alex quickly drafting in Mark Bosnich to fill the gap, it's certain that Manchester United will not easily relinquish their Premiership or European Crowns.

F.A. CUP COMPETITION

1974/75 SEASON
3rd Round
Jan 4 vs Walsall (h) 0-0
Att: 43,353
Replay
Jan 7 vs Walsall (a) 2-3 (aet.)
Att: 18,105   Daly (pen), McIlroy

1975/76 SEASON
3rd Round
Jan 3 vs Oxford United (h) 2-1
Att: 41,082   Daly 2 (2 pens)
4th Round
Jan 24 vs Peterborough United (h) 3-1
Att: 56,352   Forsyth, McIlroy, Hill
5th Round
Feb 14 vs Leicester City (a) 2-1
Att: 34,000   Macari, Daly
6th Round
Mar 6 vs Wolverhampton Wanderers (h) 1-1
Att: 59,433   Daly
Replay
Mar 9 vs Wol'hampton Wands. (a) 3-2 (aet.)
Att: 44,373   Pearson, Greenhoff, McIlroy
Semi-Final (at Hillsborough)
Apr 3 vs Derby County 2-0
Att: 55,000   Hill 2
FINAL (at Wembley)
May 1 vs Southampton 0-1
Att: 100,000

1976/77 SEASON
3rd Round
Jan 8 vs Walsall (h) 1-0
Att: 48,870   Hill
4th Round
Jan 29 vs Queen's Park Rangers (h) 1-0
Att: 57,422   Macari
5th Round
Feb 26 vs Southampton (a) 2-2
Att: 29,137   Macari, Hill
Replay
Mar 8 vs Southampton (h) 2-1
Att: 58,103   Greenhoff J 2
6th Round
Mar 19 vs Aston Villa (h) 2-1
Att: 57,089   Houston, Macari
Semi-Final (at Hillsborough)
Apr 23 vs Leeds United 2-1
Att: 55,000   Greenhoff J, Coppell
FINAL (at Wembley)
May 21 vs Liverpool 2-1
Att: 100,000   Pearson, Greenhoff J

1977/78 SEASON
3rd Round
Jan 7 vs Carlisle United (a) 1-1
Att: 25,500   Macari
Replay
Jan 11 vs Carlisle United (h) 4-2
Att: 54,156   Macari 2, Pearson 2
4th Round
Jan 28 vs West Bromwich Albion (h) 1-1
Att: 57,056   Coppell
Replay
Feb 1 vs West Bromwich Alb. (a) 2-3 (aet.)
Att: 38,000   Pearson, Hill

1978/79 SEASON
3rd Round
Jan 15 vs Chelsea (h) 3-0
Att: 38,500   Coppell, Grimes, Greenhoff J

4th Round
Jan 31 vs Fulham (a) 1-1
Att: 25,229   Greenhoff J
Replay
Feb 12 vs Fulham (h) 1-0
Att: 41,020   Greenhoff J
5th Round
Feb 20 vs Colchester United (a) 1-0
Att: 13,171   Greenhoff J
6th Round
Mar 10 vs Tottenham Hotspur (a) 1-1
Att: 51,800   Thomas
Replay
Mar 14 vs Tottenham Hotspur (h) 2-0
Att: 54,510   Jordan, McIlroy
Semi-Final (at Maine Road)
Mar 31 vs Liverpool 2-2
Att: 52,584   Jordan, Greenhoff J
Replay (at Goodison Park)
Apr 4 vs Liverpool 1-0
Att: 53,069   Greenhoff J
FINAL (at Wembley)
May 12 vs Arsenal 2-3
Att: 100,000   McQueen, McIlroy

1979/80 SEASON
3rd Round
Jan 5 vs Tottenham Hotspur (a) 1-1
Att: 45,207   McIlroy (pen)
Replay
Jan 9 vs Tottenham Hotspur (h) 0-1 (aet.)
Att: 53,762

1980/81 SEASON
3rd Round
Jan 3 vs Brighton & Hove Albion (h) 2-2
Att: 42,199   Duxbury, Thomas
Replay
Jan 7 vs Brighton & Hove Albion (a) 2-0
Att: 26,928   Nicholl, Birtles
4th Round
Jan 24 vs Nottingham Forest (a) 0-1
Att: 34,110

1981/82 SEASON
3rd Round
Jan 2 vs Watford (a) 0-1
Att: 26,104

1982/83 SEASON
3rd Round
Jan 8 vs West Ham United (h) 2-0
Att: 44,143   Coppell, Stapleton
4th Round
Jan 29 vs Luton Town (a) 2-0
Att: 20,516   Moses, Moran
5th Round
Feb 19 vs Derby County (a) 1-0
Att: 33,022   Whiteside
6th Round
Mar 12 vs Everton (h) 1-0
Att: 58,198   Stapleton
Semi-Final (at Villa Park)
Apr 16 vs Arsenal 2-1
Att: 46,535   Robson, Whiteside
FINAL (at Wembley)
May 21 vs Brighton & Hove Alb. 2-2 (aet.)
Att: 100,000   Stapleton, Wilkins
Replay (at Wembley)
May 26 vs Brighton & Hove Albion 4-0
Att: 100,000   Robson 2, Whiteside, Muhren (pen)

1983/84 SEASON
3rd Round
Jan 7 vs Bournemouth (a) 0-2
Att: 15,000

1984/85 SEASON
3rd Round
Jan 5 vs Bournemouth (h) 3-0
Att: 32,080   Strachan, McQueen, Stapleton
4th Round
Jan 26 vs Coventry City (h) 2-1
Att: 38,039   Hughes, McGrath
5th Round
Feb 15 vs Blackburn Rovers (a) 2-0
Att: 22,692   Strachan, McGrath
6th Round
Mar 9 vs West Ham United (h) 4-2
Att: 46,769   Hughes, Whiteside 3 (1 pen)
Semi-Final (at Villa Park)
Apr 13 vs Liverpool 2-2
Att: 51,690   Robson, Stapleton
Semi-Final Replay (at Maine Road)
Apr 17 vs Liverpool 2-1
Att: 45,775   Robson, Hughes
FINAL (at Wembley)
May 18 vs Everton 1-0 (aet) (90 mins 0-0)
Att: 100,000   Whiteside

1985/86 SEASON
3rd Round
Jan 9 vs Rochdale (h) 2-0
Att: 38,500   Stapleton, Hughes
4th Round
Jan 25 vs Sunderland (a) 0-0
Att: 35,484
Replay
Jan 29 vs Sunderland (h) 3-0
Att: 43,402   Whiteside, Olsen 2 (1 pen)
5th Round
Mar 5 vs West Ham United (a) 1-1
Att: 26,441   Stapleton
Replay
Mar 9 vs West Ham United (h) 0-2
Att: 30,441

1986/87 SEASON
3rd Round
Jan 10 vs Manchester City (h) 1-0
Att: 54,294   Whiteside
4th Round
Jan 31 vs Coventry City (h) 0-1
Att: 49,082

1987/88 SEASON
3rd Round
Jan 10 vs Ipswich Town (a) 2-1
Att: 23,012   D'Avray (og), Anderson
4th Round
Jan 30 vs Chelsea (h) 2-0
Att: 50,716   Whiteside, McClair
5th Round
Feb 20 vs Arsenal (a) 1-2
Att: 32,222   McClair

1988/89 SEASON
3rd Round
Jan 7 vs Queens Park Rangers (h) 0-0
Att: 36,222
Replay
Jan 11 vs Queens Park Rangers (a) 2-2 (aet.)
Att: 22,236   Gill, Graham
2nd Replay
Jan 23 vs Queens Park Rangers (h) 3-0
Att: 46,257   McClair 2 (1 pen), Robson
4th Round
Jan 28 vs Oxford United (h) 4-0
Att: 47,754   Hughes, Bruce, Phillips J (og), Robson
5th Round
Feb 18 vs Bournemouth (a) 1-1
Att: 12,500   Hughes

13

Replay
Feb 22 vs Bournemouth (h) 1-0
Att: 52,422 McClair

6th Round
Mar 18 vs Nottingham Forest (h) 0-1
Att: 55,052

1989/90 SEASON
3rd Round
Jan 7 vs Nottingham Forest (a) 1-0
Att: 23,072 Robins

4th Round
Jan 28 vs Hereford United (a) 1-0
Att: 13,777 Blackmore

5th Round
Feb 18 vs Newcastle United (a) 3-2
Att: 31,748 Robins, Wallace, McClair

6th Round
Mar 11 vs Sheffield United (a) 1-0
Att: 34,344 McClair

Semi-Final (at Maine Road)
Apr 8 vs Oldham Athletic 3-3 (aet.)
Att: 44,026 Robson, Webb, Wallace

Replay (at Maine Road)
Apr 11 vs Oldham Athletic 2-1 (aet.)
Att: 35,005 McClair, Robins

FINAL (at Wembley)
May 12 vs Crystal Palace 3-3 (aet.)
Att: 80,000 Robson, Hughes 2

REPLAY (at Wembley)
May 17 vs Crystal Palace 1-0
Att: 80,000 Martin

1990/91 SEASON
3rd Round
Jan 7 vs Queens Park Rangers (h) 2-1
Att: 35,065 Hughes, McClair

4th Round
Jan 26 vs Bolton Wanderers (h) 1-0
Att: 43,293 Hughes

5th Round
Feb 18 vs Norwich City (a) 1-2
Att: 23,058 McClair

1991/92 SEASON
3rd Round
Jan 15 vs Leeds United (a) 1-0
Att: 31,819 Hughes

4th Round
Jan 27 vs Southampton (a) 0-0
Att: 19,506

Replay
Feb 5 vs Southampton (h) 2-2 (aet.)
Att: 33,414 Kanchelskis, McClair
Southampton won 4-2 on penalties

1992/93 SEASON
3rd Round
Jan 5 vs Bury (h) 2-0
Att: 30,668 Phelan, Gillespie

4th Round
Jan 23 vs Brighton & Hove Albion (h) 1-0
Att: 33,610 Giggs

5th Round
Jan 14 vs Sheffield United (a) 1-2
Att: 27,150 Giggs

1993/94 SEASON
3rd Round
Jan 9 vs Sheffield United (a) 1-0
Att: 22,019 Hughes

4th Round
Jan 30 vs Norwich City (a) 2-0
Att: 21,060 Keane, Cantona

5th Round
Feb 20 vs Wimbledon (a) 3-0
Att: 27,511 Irwin, Cantona, Ince

6th Round
Mar 12 vs Charlton Athletic (h) 3-1
Att: 44,347 Kanchelskis 2, Hughes

Semi-Final (at Wembley)
Apr 10 vs Oldham Athletic 1-1
Att: 56,399 Hughes

Replay (at Maine Road)
Apr 13 vs Oldham Athletic 4-1
Att: 32,311 Irwin, Kanchelskis, Robson, Giggs

FINAL (at Wembley)
May 14 vs Chelsea 4-0
Att: 79,634 Cantona 2 (2 pens), Hughes, McClair

1994/95 SEASON
3rd Round
Jan 9 vs Sheffield United (a) 2-0
Att: 22,322 Hughes, Cantona

4th Round
Jan 28 vs Wrexham (h) 5-2
Att: 43,222 Irwin 2 (1 pen), Giggs, McClair, Humes (og)

5th Round
Feb 19 vs Leeds United (h) 3-1
Att: 42,744 Bruce, McClair, Hughes

6th Round
Mar 12 vs Queen's Park Rangers (h) 2-0
Att: 42,830 Irwin, Sharpe

Semi-Final (at Villa Park)
Apr 9 vs Crystal Palace 2-2 (aet.)
Att: 38,256 Irwin, Pallister

Replay (at Villa Park)
Apr 12 vs Crystal Palace 2-0
Att: 17,987 Bruce, Pallister

FINAL (at Wembley)
May 20 vs Everton 0-1
Att: 79,592

1995/96 SEASON
3rd Round
Jan 6 vs Sunderland (h) 2-2
Att: 41,563 Butt, Cantona

Replay
Jan 16 vs Sunderland (a) 2-1
Att: 21,378 Scholes, Cole

4th Round
Jan 27 vs Reading (a) 3-0
Att: 14,780 Giggs, Parker, Cantona

5th Round
Feb 18 vs Manchester City (h) 2-1
Att: 42,692 Cantona (pen), Sharpe

6th Round
Mar 11 vs Southampton (h) 2-0
Att: 45,446 Cantona, Sharpe

Semi-Final (at Villa Park)
Mar 31 vs Chelsea 2-1
Att: 38,421 Cole, Beckham

FINAL (at Wembley)
May 11 vs Liverpool 1-0
Att: 79,007 Cantona

1996/97 SEASON
3rd Round
Jan 5 vs Tottenham Hotspur (h) 2-0
Att: 52,495 Scholes, Beckham

4th Round
Jan 25 vs Wimbledon (h) 1-1
Att: 53,342 Scholes

Replay
Feb 4 vs Wimbledon (a) 0-1
Att: 25,601

1997/98 SEASON
3rd Round
Jan 4 vs Chelsea (a) 5-3
Att: 34,792 Beckham 2, Cole 2, Sheringham

4th Round
Jan 24 vs Walsall (h) 5-1
Att: 54,669 Cole 2, Solskjaer 2, Johnsen

5th Round
Feb 15 vs Barnsley (h) 1-1
Att: 54,700 Sheringham

Replay
Feb 25 vs Barnsley (a) 2-3
Att: 18,655 Sheringham, Cole

1998/99 SEASON
3rd Round
Jan 3 vs Middlesbrough (h) 3-1
Att: 52,232 Cole, Irwin (pen), Giggs

4th Round
Jan 24 vs Liverpool (h) 2-1
Att: 54,591 Yorke, Solskjaer

5th Round
Feb 14 vs Fulham (h) 1-0
Att: 54,798 Fulham

6th Round
Mar 7 vs Chelsea (h) 0-0
Att: 54,587

Replay
Mar 10 vs Chelsea (a) 2-0
Att: 33,075 Yorke 2

Semi-Final (at Villa Park)
Apr 11 vs Arsenal 0-0 (aet.)
Att: 39,217

Semi-Final Replay (at Villa Park)
Apr 14 vs Arsenal 2-1 (aet.)
Att: 30,223 Beckham, Giggs

FINAL (at Wembley)
May 22 vs Newcastle United 2-0
Att: 79,101 Sheringham, Scholes

LEAGUE CUP COMPETITION

1974/75 SEASON
2nd Round
Sep 11 vs Charlton Athletic (h) 5-1
Att: 21,616 Macari 2, McIlroy, Houston, Warman (og)

3rd Round
Oct 9 vs Manchester City (h) 1-0
Att: 55,225 Daly (pen)

4th Round
Nov 13 vs Burnley (h) 3-2
Att: 46,269 Macari 2, Morgan

5th Round
Dec 4 vs Middlesbrough (a) 0-0
Att: 36,000

Replay
Dec 18 vs Middlesbrough (h) 3-0
Att: 49,527 Pearson, McIlroy, Macari

Semi-Final (1st leg)
Jan 15 vs Norwich City (h) 2-2
Att: 58,010 Macari 2

Semi-Final (2nd leg)
Jan 22 vs Norwich City (a) 0-1 (agg. 2-3)
Att: 31,672

1975/76 SEASON
2nd Round
Sep 10 vs Brentford (h) 2-1
Att: 25,286 Macari, McIlroy

3rd Round
Oct 8 vs Aston Villa (a) 2-1
Att: 41,447 Macari, Coppell

4th Round
Nov 12 vs Manchester City (a) 0-4
Att: 50,182

1976/77 SEASON
2nd Round
Sep 1 vs Tranmere Rovers (h) 5-0
Att: 37,810   Daly 2, Macari, Pearson, Hill
3rd Round
Sep 22 vs Sunderland (h) 2-2
Att: 46,170   Pearson, Clarke (og)
Replay
Oct 4 vs Sunderland (a) 2-2 (aet.)
Att: 30,831   Greenhoff, Daly (pen)
2nd Replay
Oct 6 vs Sunderland (h) 1-0
Att: 47,689   Greenhoff
4th Round
Oct 27 vs Newcastle United (h) 7-2
*Att: 52,002   Houston, Hill 3, Pearson,
Nicholl, Coppell*
5th Round
Dec 1 vs Everton (h) 0-3
Att: 57,738

1977/78 SEASON
2nd Round
Aug 30 vs Arsenal (a) 2-3
Att: 36,161   McCreery, Pearson

1978/79 SEASON
2nd Round (played at Old Trafford)
Aug 30 vs Stockport County (a) 3-2
*Att: 42,384   Jordan, McIlroy, Greenhoff J
(pen)*
3rd Round
Oct 4 vs Watford (h) 1-2
Att: 40,534   Jordan

1979/80 SEASON
2nd Round (1st leg)
Aug 29 vs Tottenham Hotspur (a) 1-2
Att: 29,162   Thomas
2nd Round (2nd leg)
Sep 5 vs Tott. Hotspur (h) 3-1 (agg. 4-3)
Att: 48,292   Thomas, Coppell, Miller (og)
3rd Round
Sep 26 vs Norwich City (a) 1-4
Att: 18,312   McIlroy

1980/81 SEASON
2nd Round (1st leg)
Aug 27 vs Coventry City (h) 0-1
Att: 31,656
2nd Round (2nd leg)
Sep 2 vs Coventry City (a) 0-1 (agg. 0-2)
Att: 18,705

1981/82 SEASON
2nd Round (1st leg)
Oct 7 vs Tottenham Hotspur (a) 0-1
Att: 39,333
2nd Round (2nd leg)
Oct 28 vs Tott. Hotspur (h) 0-1 (agg. 0-2)
Att: 55,890

1982/83 SEASON
2nd Round (1st leg)
Oct 6 vs Bournemouth (h) 2-0
Att: 22,091   Redknapp (og), Stapleton
2nd Round (2nd leg)
Oct 26 vs Bournemouth (a) 2-2 (agg. 4-2)
Att: 13,226   Muhren, Coppell (pen)
3rd Round
Nov 10 vs Bradford City (a) 0-0
Att: 15,568
Replay
Nov 24 vs Bradford City (h) 4-1
*Att: 24,507   Moses, Albiston, Moran,
Coppell*
4th Round
Dec 1 vs Southampton (h) 2-0
Att: 28,378   McQueen, Whiteside

5th Round
Jan 19 vs Nottingham Forest (h) 4-0
Att: 44,400   McQueen 2, Coppell, Robson
Semi-Final (1st leg)
Feb 15 vs Arsenal (a) 4-2
Att: 43,136   Whiteside, Stapleton, Coppell 2
Semi-Final (2nd leg)
Feb 23 vs Arsenal (h) 2-1 (aggregate 6-3)
Att: 56,635   Coppell, Moran
FINAL (at Wembley)
Mar 26 vs Liverpool 1-2 (aet.)
Att: 100,000   Whiteside

1983/84 SEASON
2nd Round (1st leg)
Oct 3 vs Port Vale (a) 1-0
Att: 19,855   Stapleton
2nd Round (2nd leg)
Oct 26 vs Port Vale (h) 2-0 (aggregate 3-0)
Att: 23,589   Whiteside, Wilkins (pen)
3rd Round
Nov 8 vs Colchester United (a) 2-0
Att: 13,031   McQueen, Moses
4th Round
Nov 30 vs Oxford United (a) 1-1
Att: 13,711   Hughes
Replay
Dec 7 vs Oxford United (h) 1-1 (aet.)
Att: 27,459   Stapleton
2nd Replay
Dec 19 vs Oxford United (a) 1-2 (aet.)
Att: 13,912   Graham

1984/85 SEASON
2nd Round (1st leg)
Sep 26 vs Burnley (h) 4-0
Att: 28,283   Robson, Hughes 3
2nd Round (2nd leg)
Oct 9 vs Burnley (a) 3-0 (aggregate 7-0)
Att: 12,684   Brazil 2, Olsen
3rd Round
Oct 30 vs Everton (h) 1-2
Att: 50,918   Brazil

1985/86 SEASON
2nd Round (1st leg)
Sep 24 vs Crystal Palace (a) 1-0
Att: 21,506   Barnes
2nd Round (2nd leg)
Oct 7 vs Crystal Palace (h) 1-0 (agg. 2-0)
Att: 26,118   Whiteside
3rd Round
Oct 29 vs West Ham United (h) 1-0
Att: 32,057   Whiteside
4th Round
Nov 26 vs Liverpool (a) 1-2
Att: 41,291   McGrath

1986/87 SEASON
2nd Round (1st leg)
Sep 24 vs Port Vale (h) 2-0
Att: 18,906   Stapleton, Whiteside
2nd Round (2nd leg)
Oct 7 vs Port vale (a) 5-2 (aggregate 7-2)
*Att: 10,486   Stapleton, Barnes, Moses 2,
Davenport (pen)*
3rd Round
Oct 29 vs Southampton (h) 0-0
Att: 23,639
Replay
Nov 4 vs Southampton (a) 1-4
Att: 17,915   Davenport

1987/88 SEASON
2nd Round (1st leg)
Sep 23 vs Hull City (h) 5-0
*Att: 25,041   McGrath, Davenport,
Whiteside, Strachan, McClair*

2nd Round (2nd leg)
Oct 7 vs Hull City (a) 1-0 (aggregate 6-0)
Att: 13,586   McClair
3rd Round
Oct 28 vs Crystal Palace (h) 2-1
Att: 27,283   McClair 2 (1 pen)
4th Round (at Old Trafford)
Nov 18 vs Bury (a) 2-1
Att: 33,519   Whiteside, McClair
Quarter-Final
Jan 20 vs Oxford United (a) 0-2
Att: 12,658

1988/89 SEASON
2nd Round (1st leg)
Sep 28 vs Rotherham United (a) 1-0
Att: 12,592   Davenport
2nd Round (2nd leg)
Oct 12 vs Rotherham Utd. (h) 5-0 (agg 6-0)
Att: 20,597   McClair 3, Robson, Bruce
3rd Round
Nov 2 vs Wimbledon (a) 1-2
Att: 10,864   Robson

1989/90 SEASON
2nd Round (1st leg)
Sep 20 vs Portsmouth (a) 3-2
Att: 18,072   Ince 2, Wallace
2nd Round (2nd leg)
Oct 3 vs Portsmouth (h) 0-0 (aggregate 3-2)
Att: 26,698
3rd Round
Oct 25 vs Tottenham Hotspur (h) 0-3
Att: 45,759

1990/91 SEASON
2nd Round (1st leg)
Sep 26 vs Halifax Town (a) 3-1
Att: 7,500   Blackmore, McClair, Webb
2nd Round (2nd leg)
Oct 10 vs Halifax Town (h) 2-1 (agg. 5-2)
Att: 22,295   Bruce (pen), Anderson
3rd Round
Oct 31 vs Liverpool (h) 3-1
Att: 42,033   Bruce (pen), Hughes, Sharpe
4th Round
Nov 28 vs Arsenal (a) 6-2
*Att: 40,884   Blackmore, Hughes, Sharpe 3,
Wallace*
Quarter-Final
Jan 16 vs Southampton (a) 1-1
Att: 21,011   Hughes
Replay
Jan 23 vs Southampton (h) 3-2
Att: 41,093   Hughes 3
Semi-Final (1st leg)
Feb 10 vs Leeds United (h) 2-1
Att: 34,050   Sharpe, McClair
Semi-Final (2nd leg)
Feb 24 vs Leeds United (a) 1-0 (agg. 3-1)
Att: 32,014   Sharpe
FINAL (at Wembley)
Apr 21 vs Sheffield Wednesday 0-1
Att: 80,000

1991/92 SEASON
2nd Round (1st leg)
Sep 25 vs Cambridge United (h) 3-0
Att: 30,934   Giggs, McClair, Bruce
2nd Round (2nd leg)
Oct 9 vs Cambridge United (a) 1-1 (agg 4-1)
Att: 9,248   McClair
3rd Round
Oct 30 vs Portsmouth (h) 3-1
Att: 29,543   Robins 2, Robson

15

4th Round
Dec 4 vs Oldham Athletic (h) 2-0
Att: 38,550   McClair, Kanchelskis

Quarter-Final
Jan 8 vs Leeds United (a) 3-1
Att: 28,886   Blackmore, Kanchelskis, Giggs

Semi-Final (1st leg)
Mar 4 vs Middlesbrough (a) 0-0
Att: 25,572

Semi-Final (2nd leg)
Mar 11 vs Middlesbrough (h) 2-1 (agg. 2-1)
Att: 45,875   Sharpe, Giggs

FINAL (at Wembley)
Apr 12 vs Nottingham Forest 1-0
Att: 76,810   McClair

1992/93 SEASON
2nd Round (1st leg)
Sep 23 vs Brighton & Hove Albion (a) 1-1
Att: 16,649   Wallace

2nd Round (2nd leg)
Oct 7 vs Brighton & H.A. (h) 1-0 (agg. 2-1)
Att: 25,405   Hughes

3rd Round
Oct 28 vs Aston Villa (a) 0-1
Att: 35,964

1993/94 SEASON
2nd Round (1st leg)
Sep 22 vs Stoke City (a) 1-2
Att: 23,327   Dublin

2nd Round (2nd leg)
Oct 6 vs Stoke City (h) 2-0 (aggregate 3-2)
Att: 41,387   Sharpe, McClair

3rd Round
Oct 27 vs Leicester City (h) 5-1
Att: 41,344   Bruce 2, Sharpe, McClair, Hughes

4th Round
Nov 30 vs Everton (a) 2-0
Att: 34,052   Hughes, Giggs

Quarter-Final
Jan 12 vs Portsmouth (h) 2-2
Att: 43,794   Cantona, Giggs

Replay
Jan 26 vs Portsmouth (a) 1-0
Att: 24,950   McClair

Semi-Final (1st leg)
Feb 13 vs Sheffield Wednesday (h) 1-0
Att: 43,294   Giggs

Semi-Final (2nd leg)
Mar 2 vs Sheff. Wednesday (a) 4-1 (agg 5-1)
Att: 34,878   Kanchelskis, McClair, Hughes 2

FINAL (at Wembley)
Mar 27 vs Aston Villa 1-3
Att: 77,231   Hughes

1994/95 SEASON
2nd Round (1st leg)
Sep 21 vs Port Vale (a) 2-1
Att: 18,605   Scholes 2

2nd Round (2nd leg)
Oct 5 vs Port Vale (h) 2-0 (aggregate 4-1)
Att: 31,615   McClair, May

3rd Round
Oct 26 vs Newcastle United (a) 0-2
Att: 34,178

1995/96 SEASON
2nd Round (1st leg)
Sep 20 vs York City (h) 0-3
Att: 29,049

2nd Round (2nd leg)
Oct 3 vs York City (a) 3-1 (aggregate 3-4)
Att: 9,386   Scholes 2, Cooke

1996/97 SEASON
3rd Round
Oct 23 vs Swindon Town (h) 2-1
Att: 49,305   Poborsky, Scholes

4th Round
Nov 27 vs Leicester City (a) 0-2
Att: 20,428

1997/98 SEASON
3rd Round
Oct 14 vs Ipswich Town (a) 0-2
Att: 22,173

1998/99 SEASON
3rd Round
Oct 28 vs Bury (h) 2-0 (aet.)
Att: 52,495   Solskjaer, Nevland

4th Round
Nov 11 vs Nottingham Forest (h) 2-1
Att: 37,237   Solskjaer 2

5th Round
Dec 2 vs Tottenham Hotspur (a) 1-3
Att: 35,702   Sheringham

EUROPEAN CHAMPIONS CUP
1993/94 SEASON
1st Round (1st leg)
Sep 15 vs Honved (a) 3-2
Att: 9,000   Cantona, Keane 2

1st Round (2nd leg)
Sep 29 vs Honved (h) 2-1 (aggregate 5-3)
Att: 35,781   Bruce 2

2nd Round (1st leg)
Oct 20 vs Galatasaray (h) 3-3
Att: 39,346   Robson, Hakan (og), Cantona

2nd Round (2nd leg)
Nov 3 vs Galatasaray (a) 0-0 (aggreg. 3-3)
Att: 40,000
Galatasaray won on Away Goals

1994/95 SEASON
Group A, Game One
Sep 14 vs IFK Gothenburg (h) 4-2
Att: 33,625   Giggs 2, Kanchelskis, Sharpe

Group A, Game Two
Sep 28 vs Galatasaray (a) 0-0
Att: 35,000

Group A, Game Three
Oct 19 vs Barcelona (h) 2-2
Att: 40,064   Hughes, Sharpe

Group A, Game Four
Nov 2 vs Barcelona (a) 0-4
Att: 114,432

Group A, Game Five
Nov 23 vs IFK Gothenburg (a) 1-3
Att: 36,350   Hughes

Group A, Game Six
Dec 7 vs Galatasaray (h) 4-0
Att: 39,220   Davies, Beckham, Keane, Bulent (og)

1996/97 SEASON
Group C, Game One
Sep 11 vs Juventus (a) 0-1
Att: 50,000

Group C, Game Two
Sep 25 vs Rapid Vienna (h) 2-0
Att: 51,831   Solskjaer, Beckham

Group C, Game Three
Oct 16 vs Fenerbahce (a) 2-0
Att: 26,200   Beckham, Cantona

Group C, Game Four
Oct 30 vs Fenerbahce (h) 0-1
Att: 53,297

Group C, Game Five
Nov 20 vs Juventus (a) 0-1
Att: 53,529

Group C, Game Six
Dec 4 vs Rapid Vienna (a) 2-0
Att: 45,000   Giggs, Cantona

Quarter-Final (1st leg)
Mar 5 vs Porto (h) 4-0
Att: 53,415   May, Cantona, Giggs, Cole

Quarter-Final (2nd leg)
Mar 19 vs Porto (a) 0-0 (aggregate 4-0)
Att: 40,000

Semi-Final (1st leg)
Apr 9 vs Borussia Dortmund (a) 0-1
Att: 48,500

Semi-Final (2nd leg)
Apr 23 vs Bor. Dortmund (h) 0-1 (agg. 0-2)
Att: 53,606

1997/98 SEASON
Group B, Game One
Sep 17 vs Kosice (a) 3-0
Att: 10,000   Irwin, Berg, Cole

Group B, Game Two
Oct 1 vs Juventus (h) 3-2
Att: 53,428   Sheringham, Scholes, Giggs

Group B, Game Three
Oct 22 vs Feyenoord (h) 2-1
Att: 53,188   Scholes, Irwin (pen)

Group B, Game Four
Nov 5 vs Feyenoord (a) 3-1
Att; 45,000   Cole 3

Group B, Game Five
Nov 27 vs Kosice (h) 3-0
Att: 53,535   Cole, Faktor (og), Sheringham

Group B, Game Six
Dec 10 vs Juventus (a) 0-1
Att: 47,786

Quarter-Final (1st leg)
Mar 4 vs Monaco (a) 0-0
Att: 15,000

Quarter-Final (2nd leg)
Mar 18 vs Monaco (h) 1-1 (aggregate 1-1)
Att: 53,683   Solskjaer
Monaco won on Away Goals

1998/99 SEASON
2nd Qualifying Round (1st leg)
Aug 12 vs LKS Lodz (h) 2-0
Att: 50,906   Giggs, Cole

2nd Qualifying Round (2nd leg)
Aug 26 vs LKS Lodz (a) 0-0 (aggreg. 2-0)
Att: 8,000

Group D, Game One
Sep 16 vs Barcelona (h) 3-3
Att: 53,601   Giggs, Scholes, Beckham

Group D, Game Two
Sep 30 vs Bayern Munich (a) 2-2
Att: 57,000   Yorke, Scholes

Group D, Game Three
Oct 21 vs Brondby (a) 6-2
Att: 40,530   Giggs 2, Cole, Keane, Yorke, Solskjaer

Group D, Game Four
Nov 4 vs Brondby (h) 5-0
Att: 53,250   Beckham, Cole, Neville P, Yorke, Scholes

Group D, Game Five
Nov 25 vs Barcelona (a) 3-3
Att: 67,650   Yorke 2, Cole

Group D, Game Six
Dec 9 vs Bayern Munich (h) 1-1
Att: 54,434   Keane

Quarter-Final (1st leg)
Mar 3 vs Internazionale (h) 2-0
Att: 54,430   Yorke 2

Quarter-Final (2nd leg)
Mar 17 vs Internazionale (a) 1-1 (agg. 3-1)
Att: 79,528   Scholes

Semi-Final (1st leg)
Apr 7 vs Juventus (h) 1-1
Att: 54,487   Giggs

Semi-Final (2nd leg)
Apr 21 vs Juventus (a) 3-2 (aggregate 4-3)
Att: 65,500   Keane, Yorke, Cole

FINAL (Nou Camp Stadium, Barcelona)
May 26 vs Bayern Munich 2-1
Att: 90,000   Sheringham, Solskjaer

EUROPEAN CUP-WINNERS CUP

1977/78 SEASON
1st Round (1st leg)
Sep 14 vs St. Etienne (a) 1-1
Att: 33,678   Hill

1st Round (2nd leg) (played at Plymouth)
Oct 5 vs St. Etienne (h) 2-0 (aggregate 3-1)
Att: 31,634   Pearson, Coppell

2nd Round (1st leg)
Oct 19 vs Porto (a) 0-4
Att: 40,000

2nd Round (2nd leg)
Nov 2 vs Porto (h) 5-2 (aggregate 5-6)
Att: 52,375   Coppell 2, Murca 2 (2 ogs), Nicholl

1983/84 SEASON
1st Round (1st leg)
Sep 14 vs Dukla Prague (h) 1-1
Att: 39,765   Wilkins (pen)

1st Round (2nd leg)
Sep 27 vs Dukla Prague (a) 2-2 (agg. 3-3)
Att: 25,000   Robson, Whiteside
Manchester United won on Away Goals

2nd Round (1st leg)
Oct 19 vs Spartak Varna (a) 2-1
Att: 37,500   Robson (pen), Graham

2nd Round (2nd leg)
Nov 2 vs Spartak Varna (h) 2-0 (agg. 4-1)
Att: 39,079   Stapleton 2

Quarter-Final (1st leg)
Mar 7 vs Barcelona (a) 0-2
Att: 90,000

Quarter-Final (2nd leg)
Mar 21 vs Barcelona (h) 3-0 (aggreg. 3-2)
Att: 58,350   Robson 2, Stapleton

Semi-Final (1st leg)
Apr 11 vs Juventus (h) 1-1
Att: 58,231   Davies

Semi-Final (2nd leg)
Apr 25 vs Juventus (a) 1-2 (aggregate 2-3)
Att: 70,000   Whiteside

1990/91 SEASON
1st Round (1st leg)
Sep 19 vs Pecsi Munkas (h) 2-0
Att: 26,411   Blackmore, Webb

1st Round (2nd leg)
Oct 3 vs Pecsi Munkas (a) 1-0 (agg. 3-0)
Att: 15,000   McClair

2nd Round (1st leg)
Oct 23 vs Wrexham (h) 3-0
Att: 29,405   McClair, Bruce (pen), Pallister

2nd Round (2nd leg)
Nov 7 vs Wrexham (a) 2-0 (aggregate 5-0)
Att: 13,327   Robins, Bruce

Quarter-Final (1st leg)
Mar 6 vs Montpellier (h) 1-1
Att: 41,942   McClair

Quarter-Final (2nd leg)
Mar 19 vs Montpellier (a) 2-0 (agg. 3-1)
Att: 20,500   Blackmore, Bruce (pen)

Semi-Final (1st leg)
Apr 10 vs Legia Warsaw (a) 3-1
Att: 17,500   McClair, Hughes, Bruce

Semi-Final (2nd leg)
Apr 24 vs Legia Warsaw (h) 1-1 (agg. 4-2)
Att: 44,269   Sharpe

FINAL (in Rotterdam)
May 15 vs Barcelona 2-1
Att: 45,000   Hughes 2

1991/92 SEASON
1st Round (1st leg)
Sep 18 vs Athinaikos (a) 0-0
Att: 9,500

1st Round (2nd leg)
Oct 2 vs Athinaikos (h) 2-0 (aet.) (agg. 2-0)
Att: 35,023   Hughes, McClair

2nd Round (1st leg)
Oct 23 vs Atletico Madrid (a) 0-3
Att: 52,000

2nd Round (2nd leg)
Nov 6 vs Atletico Madrid (h) 1-1 (agg. 1-4)
Att: 39,654   Hughes

UEFA CUP

1976/77 SEASON
1st Round (1st leg)
Sep 15 vs Ajax (a) 0-1
Att: 22,000

1st Round (2nd leg)
Sep 29 vs Ajax (h) 2-0 (aggregate 2-1)
Att: 58,938   Macari, McIlroy

2nd Round (1st leg)
Oct 20 vs Juventus (h) 1-0
Att: 59,021

2nd Round (2nd leg)
Nov 3 vs Juventus (a) 0-3 (aggregate 1-3)
Att: 65,000

1980/81 SEASON
1st Round (1st leg)
Sep 17 vs Widzew Lodz (h) 1-1
Att: 38,037   McIlroy

1st Round (2nd leg)
Oct 1 vs Widzew Lodz (a) 0-0 (agg. 1-1)
Att: 40,000
Widzew Lodz won on Away Goals

1982/83 SEASON
1st Round (1st leg)
Sep 15 vs Valencia (h) 0-0
Att: 46,599

1st Round (2nd leg)
Sep 29 vs Valencia (a) 1-2 (aggregate 1-2)
Att: 47,000   Robson

1984/85 SEASON
1st Round (1st leg)
Sep 19 vs Raba Gyor (h) 3-0
Att: 32,537   Robson, Muhren, Hughes

1st Round (2nd leg)
Oct 3 vs Raba Gyor (a) 2-2 (aggregate 5-2)
Att: 28,000   Brazil, Muhren (pen)

2nd Round (1st leg)
Oct 24 vs PSV Eindhoven (a) 0-0
Att: 26,500

2nd Round (2nd leg)
Nov 7 vs PSV Eindhoven (h) 1-0 (agg. 1-0)
Att: 39,281   Strachan (pen)

3rd Round (1st leg)
Nov 28 vs Dundee United (h) 2-2
Att: 48,278   Strachan (pen), Robson

3rd Round (2nd leg)
Dec 12 vs Dundee United (a) 3-2 (agg. 5-4)
Att: 22,500   Hughes, McGinnis (og), Muhren

Quarter-Final (1st leg)
Mar 6 vs Videoton (h) 1-0
Att: 35,432   Stapleton

Quarter-Final (2nd leg)
Mar 20 vs Videoton (a) 0-1 (aet.) (agg. 1-1)
Att: 25,000   Videoton won 5-4 on penalties

1995/96 SEASON
1st Round (1st leg)
Sep 12 vs Rotor Volgograd (a) 0-0
Att: 40,000

1st Round (2nd leg)
Sep 26 vs Rotor Volgograd (h) 2-2 (agg. 2-2)
Att: 29,724   Scholes, Schmeichel
Rotor Volgograd won on Away Goals

1974-75

1	Aug	17	(a)	Orient	W	2-0	Morgan, Houston	17,772
2		24	(h)	Millwall	W	4-0	Daly 3 (2 pens), Pearson	44,756
3		28	(h)	Portsmouth	W	2-1	Daly (pen), McIlroy	42,547
4		31	(a)	Cardiff C	W	1-0	Daly (pen)	22,344
5	Sep	7	(h)	Nottingham F	D	2-2	B. Greenhoff, McIlroy	40,671
6		14	(a)	West Brom A	D	1-1	Pearson	23,721
7		16	(a)	Millwall	W	1-0	Daly (pen)	16,988
8		21	(h)	Bristol R	W	2-0	B. Greenhoff, Prince (og)	42,948
9		25	(h)	Bolton W	W	3-0	Macari, Houston, McAllister (og)	47,084
10		28	(a)	Norwich C	L	0-2		24,586
11	Oct	5	(a)	Fulham	W	2-1	Pearson 2	26,513
12		12	(h)	Notts Co	W	1-0	McIlroy	46,565
13		15	(a)	Portsmouth	D	0-0		25,608
14		19	(a)	Blackpool	W	3-0	Forsyth, Macari, McCalliog	25,370
15		26	(h)	Southampton	W	1-0	Pearson	48,724
16	Nov	2	(h)	Oxford U	W	4-0	Pearson 3, Macari	41,909
17		9	(a)	Bristol C	L	0-1		28,104
18		16	(h)	Aston Villa	W	2-1	Daly 2 (1 pen)	55,615
19		23	(a)	Hull C	L	0-2		23,287
20		30	(h)	Sunderland	W	3-2	Pearson, Morgan, McIlroy	60,585
21	Dec	7	(a)	Sheffield W	D	4-4	Houston, Macari 2, Pearson	35,230
22		14	(h)	Orient	D	0-0		41,200
23		21	(a)	York C	W	1-0	Pearson	15,567
24		26	(h)	West Brom A	W	2-1	McIlroy, Daly (pen)	51,104
25		28	(a)	Oldham Ath	L	0-1		26,384
26	Jan	11	(h)	Sheffield W	W	2-0	McCalliog 2 (1 pen)	45,662
27		18	(a)	Sunderland	D	0-0		45,976
28	Feb	1	(h)	Bristol C	L	0-1		47,118
29		8	(a)	Oxford U	L	0-1		15,959
30		15	(h)	Hull C	W	2-0	Houston, Pearson	44,712
31		22	(a)	Aston Villa	L	0-2		39,156
32	Mar	1	(h)	Cardiff C	W	4-0	Houston, Pearson, McIlroy, Macari	43,601
33		8	(a)	Bolton W	W	1-0	Pearson	38,152
34		15	(h)	Norwich C	D	1-1	Pearson	56,202
35		22	(a)	Nottingham F	W	1-0	Daly	21,893
36		28	(a)	Bristol R	D	1-1	Macari	19,337
37		29	(h)	York C	W	2-1	Morgan, Macari	46,802
38		31	(h)	Oldham Ath	W	3-2	McIlroy, Macari, Coppell	56,618
39	Apr	5	(a)	Southampton	W	1-0	Macari	21,866
40		12	(h)	Fulham	W	1-0	Daly	52,971
41		19	(a)	Notts Co	D	2-2	Houston, B. Greenhoff	17,320
42		26	(h)	Blackpool	W	4-0	Pearson 2, Macari, B. Greenhoff	58,769

FINAL LEAGUE POSITION: 1st in Division Two

Appearances

Sub. Appearances

Goals

Appearances / line-up grid (shirt numbers by match). The column at the far right is the match number (1–42).

Stepney	Forsyth	Houston	Greenhoff B	Holton	Buchan M	Morgan	Macari	Pearson	McCalliog	Daly	McIlroy	Martin	Young	Sidebottom	Albiston	McCreery	Graham	Davies R	James	Baldwin	Roche	Coppell	Nicholl	#
1	2	3	4	5	6	7	8*	9	10	11	12													1
1	2	3	4	5	6	7		9		11	8	10												2
1	2	3	4	5	6	7		9		11	8	10												3
1	2	3	4	5	6	7		9*		11	8	10	12											4
1	2	3	4*	5	6	7	12		10	11	8	9												5
1	2	3	12	5	6	7		9	10	11	8	4*												6
1	2	3	4		6	7		9	10	11*	8		12	5										7
1	2	3	4	5	6	7		9	10*	11	8		12											8
1	2	3	4		6	7		9	10	11	8			5										9
1	2	3	4		6	7*		9	10	11	8		12	5										10
1	2	3	4	5	6	7	12	9	10	11*	8													11
1	2	3	4	5		7		9	10*	11	8		12											12
1	2		4	5	6	7*		9	10	11	8				3	12								13
1	2	3	4	5	6	7		9	10	11*	8					12								14
1	2	3	4	5	6	7*	9	12	10	11	8													15
1	2	3	4*		6	7	12	9	10	11	8			5										16
1	2	3	4		6		7	9	10	11*	8			5			12							17
1	2	3	12		6	7	4	9*	10	11	8			5										18
1	2	3	9		6	7	4		10	11	8			5										19
1	2	3	4*	5	6	7	10	9		11	8							12						20
1	2	3	4	5*	6	7	10	9	11		8							12						21
1	2	3	4*		6	7	10	9		11	8			5				12						22
1		3	4		6	7	10	9		11	8		2	5*				12						23
1		3	4		6	7	10	9		11	8		2	5				12						24
1			4*		6	7	10	9		11	8		2	5	3			12						25
1	2	3	4		6	7*	10	9	11	12	8							5						26
1	2	3	4		6	7	10		11		8							5		9				27
1	2	3			6	7	10		11	4*	8	12						5		9				28
	2	3	4		6	7*	10	9			8		11					12	5		1			29
	2	3	4		6		10	9			8	11	7					12	5*		1			30
1	2	3	4		6		10	9			8	11*	7	5				12						31
1	2	3	4		6	7*	10	9		11	8							5				12		32
1	2	3*	4		6		10	9		11	8	12						5				7		33
1	2	3	4		6		10	9		11	8	12						5				7*		34
1	2	3	4		6		10	9		11	8							5				7		35
1	2	3	4		6	12	10	9		11	8							5*				7		36
1	2	3	5		6	4	10	9		11	8											7		37
1	2	3	5		6	4	10	9		11*	8	12										7		38
1	2	3	5		6*	7	10	9		11	8	4										12		39
1	2	3	4		6		10	9		11	8							5				7		40
1	2	3	4		6		10	9		11	8							5				7		41
1	2	3	4		6		10	9		11	8							5				7		42
40	39	40	39	14	41	32	36	30	20	36	41	7	7	12	2			13	2	2	9			
			2				2	2	1		1	1	1	8		2	1	8		1	1			
	1	6	4			3	11	17	3	11	7								1					

1975-76

1	Aug	16	(a)	Wolves	W	2-0	Macari 2		32,348
2		19	(a)	Birmingham C	W	2-0	McIlroy 2		33,177
3		23	(h)	Sheffield U	W	5-1	Pearson 2, Badger (og), Daly, McIlroy		55,949
4		27	(h)	Coventry C	D	1-1	Pearson		52,169
5		30	(a)	Stoke C	W	1-0	Dodd (og)		33,092
6	Sep	6	(h)	Tottenham H	W	3-2	Pratt (og), Daly 2 (1 pen)		51,641
7		13	(a)	Q.P.R.	L	0-1			29,237
8		20	(h)	Ipswich T	W	1-0	Houston		50,513
9		24	(a)	Derby Co	L	1-2	Daly		33,187
10		27	(a)	Manchester C	D	2-2	McCreery, Macari		46,931
11	Oct	4	(h)	Leicester C	D	0-0			47,878
12		11	(a)	Leeds U	W	2-1	McIlroy 2		40,264
13		18	(h)	Arsenal	W	3-1	Coppell 2, Pearson		53,885
14		25	(a)	West Ham U	L	1-2	Macari		38,528
15	Nov	1	(h)	Norwich C	W	1-0	Pearson		50,587
16		8	(a)	Liverpool	L	1-3	Coppell		49,136
17		15	(h)	Aston Villa	W	2-0	Coppell, McIlroy		51,682
18		22	(a)	Arsenal	L	1-3	Pearson		40,102
19		29	(h)	Newcastle U	W	1-0	Daly		52,624
20	Dec	6	(a)	Middlesbrough	D	0-0			32,454
21		13	(a)	Sheffield U	W	4-1	Pearson 2, Hill, Macari		31,741
22		20	(h)	Wolves	W	1-0	Hill		44,269
23		23	(a)	Everton	D	1-1	Macari		41,732
24		27	(h)	Burnley	W	2-1	McIlroy, Macari		59,726
25	Jan	10	(h)	Q.P.R.	W	2-1	Hill, McIlroy		58,312
26		17	(a)	Tottenham H	D	1-1	Hill		49,189
27		31	(h)	Birmingham C	W	3-1	Forsyth, Macari, McIlroy		50,724
28	Feb	7	(a)	Coventry C	D	1-1	Macari		33,922
29		18	(h)	Liverpool	D	0-0			59,709
30		21	(a)	Aston Villa	L	1-2	Macari		50,094
31		25	(h)	Derby Co	D	1-1	Pearson		59,632
32		28	(h)	West Ham U	W	4-0	Forsyth, Macari, McCreery, Pearson		57,220
33	Mar	13	(h)	Leeds U	W	3-2	Houston, Pearson, Daly		59,429
34		17	(a)	Norwich C	D	1-1	Hill		27,787
35		20	(a)	Newcastle U	W	4-3	Pearson 2, Bird (og), Howard (og)		45,043
36		27	(h)	Middlesbrough	W	3-0	Daly (pen), McCreery, Hill		58,527
37	Apr	10	(a)	Ipswich T	L	0-3			34,886
38		17	(h)	Everton	W	2-1	Kenyon (og), McCreery		61,879
39		19	(a)	Burnley	W	1-0	Macari		27,418
40		21	(h)	Stoke C	L	0-1			53,879
41		24	(a)	Leicester C	L	1-2	Coyne		31,053
42	May	4	(h)	Manchester C	W	2-0	Hill, McIlroy		59,517

FINAL LEAGUE POSITION: 3rd in Division One

Appearances

Sub. Appearances

Goals

Stepney	Forsyth	Houston	Jackson	Greenhoff B	Buchan	Coppell	McIlroy	Pearson	Macari	Daly	Nicholl	McCreery	Young A	Albiston	Grimshaw	Roche	Hill	Kelly	Coyne	
1	2	3	4	5	6	7	8	9*	10	11	12									1
1	2	3	4	5*	6	7	8		10	11	12	9								2
1	2*	3	4	5	6	7	8	9	10	11	12									3
1	2	3	4	5	6	7	8	9	10	11										4
1	2	3	4	5	6	7	8	9	10	11										5
1		3	4	5	6	7	8	9	10	11	2									6
1		3	4*		6	7	8	9	10	11	2	12	5							7
1		3		5	6	7	8	9	10	11	2	4								8
1		3		5	6	7	8	9	10	11	2	4								9
1		3		5	6	7	8	9	10	11	2	4								10
1		3	4*	5	6	7	8	9	10	11	2	12								11
1		3	4	5	6	7	8	9	10	11	2				12					12
1	3*		4	5	6	7	8	9	10	11	2									13
1		3	4	5	6	7	8	9	10	11*	2	12								14
		3	4	5	6	7	8	9	10	11	2					1				15
		3	4*	5	6	7	8	9	10	11	2	12				1				16
		3		5	6	7	8*	9	10	11	2	12				1	11			17
		3		5	6	7	8*	9	10	4	2	12				1	11			18
1		3		5	6	7	8	9*	10	4	2	12					11			19
1	2*	3		5	6	7	8	9	10	4	12						11			20
1	2	3		5	6	7	8*	9	10	4		12					11			21
1	2	3		5*	6	7	8	9	10	4							11	12		22
1	2	3		5	6	7	8	9	10	4							11			23
1	2	3		5	6	7	8	9*	10	4		12					11			24
1	2	3		5	6	7	8	9	10	4							11			25
1	2	3		5	6	7	8*	9	10	4		12					11			26
1	2	3		5	6	7	8	9*	10	4		12					11			27
1	2	3		5	6	7	8	9*	10	4		12					11			28
1	2	3		5	6	7	8*	9	10	4		12					11			29
1	2	3		5	6	7	8	9*	10	4							11	12		30
1	2	3		5	6	7	8	9	10	4		12					11*			31
1	2	3		5	6	7	8*	9	10	4		12					11			32
1	2	3		5	6	7	8	9		4	10						11			33
1	2	3		5	6	7	8	9		4	10						11			34
1	2	3		5	6	7	8	9		4	10						11			35
1	2	3		5	6	7	8	9		4	10						11			36
1	2	3		5	6	7	8	9		4	10						11			37
1	2	3		5	6	7*	8	9	10	4		12					11			38
1	2	3	12	5	6		8	9*	10	4	7						11			39
1	2	3	7*	5	6		8		10	4	12	9					11			40
1	2	3*	7	5	6			10		4	8			12			11	9		41
1	2	3	10		6		8	9*		4	12			5			11			42
38	28	42	16	40	42	39	41	39	36	41	15	12		2		4	26	1		
			1								5	16	1	1	1			1	1	
	2	2				4	10	13	12	7	4						7		1	

21

1976-77

1	Aug	21	(h)	Birmingham C	D	2-2	Coppell, Pearson	58,898
2		24	(a)	Coventry C	W	2-0	Macari, Hill	26,775
3		28	(a)	Derby Co	D	0-0		30,054
4	Sep	4	(h)	Tottenham H	L	2-3	Coppell, Pearson	60,723
5		11	(a)	Newcastle U	D	2-2	B. Greenhoff, Pearson	39,037
6		18	(h)	Middlesbrough	W	2-0	McAndrew (og), Pearson	56,712
7		25	(a)	Manchester C	W	3-1	Coppell, McCreery, Daly	48,861
8	Oct	2	(a)	Leeds U	W	2-0	Daly, Coppell	44,512
9		46	(a)	West Brom A	L	0-4		36,615
10		23	(h)	Norwich C	D	2-2	Daly (pen), Hill	54,356
11		30	(h)	Ipswich T	L	0-1		57,416
12	Nov	6	(a)	Aston Villa	L	2-3	Pearson, Hill	44,789
13		10	(h)	Sunderland	D	3-3	Hill, Pearson, B. Greenhoff	42,685
14		20	(a)	Leicester C	D	1-1	Daly (pen)	26,421
15		27	(h)	West Ham U	L	0-2		55,366
16	Dec	18	(a)	Arsenal	L	1-3	McIlroy	39,572
17		27	(h)	Everton	W	4-0	Pearson, J. Greenhoff, Hill, Macari	56,786
18	Jan	1	(h)	Aston Villa	W	2-0	Pearson 2	55,446
19		3	(a)	Ipswich T	L	1-2	Pearson	30,105
20		15	(h)	Coventry C	W	2-0	Macari 2	46,567
21		19	(h)	Bristol C	W	2-1	Pearson, B. Greenhoff	43,051
22		22	(a)	Birmingham C	W	3-2	Houston, J. Greenhoff, Pearson	35,316
23	Feb	5	(h)	Derby Co	W	3-1	Macari, Houston, Powell (og)	54,044
24		12	(a)	Tottenham H	W	3-1	Macari, McIlroy, Hill	46,946
25		16	(h)	Liverpool	D	0-0		57,487
26		19	(h)	Newcastle U	W	3-1	J. Greenhoff 3	51,828
27	Mar	5	(h)	Manchester C	W	3-1	Pearson, Hill, Coppell	58,595
28		12	(h)	Leeds U	W	1-0	Cherry (og)	60,612
29		23	(h)	West Brom A	D	2-2	Hill (pen), Coppell	51,053
30	Apr	2	(a)	Norwich C	L	1-2	Powell (og)	24,161
31		5	(a)	Everton	W	2-1	Hill 2	38,216
32		9	(h)	Stoke C	W	3-0	Houston, Macari, Pearson	53,102
33		11	(a)	Sunderland	L	1-2	Hill (pen)	38,785
34		16	(h)	Leicester C	D	1-1	J. Greenhoff	49,161
35		19	(a)	Q.P.R.	L	0-4		28,848
36		26	(a)	Middlesbrough	L	0-3		21,744
37		30	(h)	Q.P.R.	W	1-0	Macari	50,788
38	May	3	(a)	Liverpool	L	0-1		53,046
39		7	(a)	Bristol C	D	1-1	J. Greenhoff (pen)	28,864
40		10	(a)	Stoke C	D	3-3	Hill 2, McCreery	24,204
41		14	(h)	Arsenal	W	3-2	J. Greenhoff, Macari, Hill	53,232
42		16	(a)	West Ham U	L	2-4	Hill, Pearson	29,904

FINAL LEAGUE POSITION: 6th in Division One

Appearances

Sub. Appearances

Goals

	Stepney	Nicholl	Houston	Daly	Greenhoff B	Buchan	Coppell	McIlroy	Pearson	Macari	Hill	Foggon	McCreery	Waldron	McGrath	Albiston	Roche	Paterson	Clark	Greenhoff J	Forsyth	Jackson	
1	1	2	3	4*	5	6	7	8	9	10	11	12											1
2	1	2	3	4	5	6	7	8	9	10	11												2
3	1	2	3	4	5	6	7	8	9	10	11												3
4	1	2	3	4	5	6	7	8*	9	10	11		12										4
5	1	2	3	4	5	6	7	8	9	10	11*	12											5
6	1	2	3	4*	5	6	7	8	9	10	11	12											6
7	1	2	3	4	5	6	7	8	9*	10	11		12										7
8	1	2	3	4	5	6	7	8	9*	10	11		12										8
9	1	2	3	4	5		7	8	9	10*	11		12	6									9
10	1	2	3	4	5		7	8*	9	10	11			6	12								10
11	1	2	6	4	5		7	8	9	10*	11		12			3							11
12	1	2	6	4	5		10	8	9		11				7	3							12
13			3	4	5		7		9	10	11		6*			2	1	5	12				13
14	1	2		4	5		7	8	9		11					3		6		10			14
15	1		6	4	5		7	8	9		11					3				10	2		15
16	1		3		5*	6		4	9	10	11		7		12					8	2		16
17	1	2	3		5	6	7*	4	9	10	11		12							8			17
18	1	2	3		5	6	7	4	9*	10	11		12							8			18
19	1	2			5	6		4	9*	10	11		7		12	3				8			19
20	1	2	3		5	6	7	4	9	10	11*		12							8			20
21	1	2	3		5	6	7	4	9	10	11									8			21
22	1	2	3	12	5	6	7	4	9	10	11*									8			22
23	1	2	3	11	5	6	7	4	9	10										8			23
24	1	2	3		5	6	7	4	9	10	11									8			24
25	1	2	3		5	6	7	4	9	10	11									8			25
26	1	2	3		5	6	7	4	9	10	11*					12				8			26
27	1	2	3		5	6	7	4	9	10	11*		12							8			27
28	1	2	3		5	6	7	4	9	10	11*		12							8			28
29	1	2			5	6	7	4*	9	10			12			3				8			29
30	1	2	3		5	6	7	4		10	11*		9	12						8			30
31	1	2	3		5	6	7	4	9		11*		10		12					8			31
32	1	2	3		5	6	7	4	9	10	11		12							8*			32
33	1	2	3		5	6	7	4	9	10*	11		8			12							33
34	1	2			5	6	7	4	9	10	12		11*			3				8			34
35	1	2	6		5*		7	4	9	10			11			3				8	12		35
36	1	2	3		5	6	7	4	9	10	11									8			36
37	1	2	3		5	6	7	4	9	10	11*		12							8			37
38	1	2	3				7	4	9	10	11		12			6				8*	5		38
39	1	2	3*		5	6	7	12		10			9		11					8		4	39
40	1	2			5	6	7			10	11		8		9	3						4	40
41	1	2			5	6	7	4	9*	10	11		12			3				8			41
42		2			5	6	7	4	9	10	11		12			3	1			8*			42
	40	39	36	16	40	33	40	39	39	38	38		9	3	2	14	2	2		27	3	2	
				1							1	3	16		4	3			1		1		
			3	4	3		6	2	15	9	15		2							8			

1977-78

1	Aug	20	(a)	Birmingham C	W	4-1	Macari 3, Hill		28,005
2		24	(h)	Coventry C	W	2-1	Hill (pen), McCreery		55,726
3		27	(h)	Ipswich T	D	0-0			57,904
4	Sep	3	(a)	Derby Co	W	1-0	Macari		21,279
5		10	(a)	Manchester C	L	1-3	Nicholl		50,856
6		17	(h)	Chelsea	L	0-1			54,951
7		24	(a)	Leeds U	D	1-1	Hill		33,507
8	Oct	1	(h)	Liverpool	W	2-0	Macari, McIlroy		55,089
9		8	(a)	Middlesbrough	L	1-2	Coppell		26,822
10		15	(h)	Newcastle U	W	3-2	Coppell, J. Greenhoff, Macari		55,056
11		22	(a)	West Brom A	L	0-1			27,526
12		29	(a)	Aston Villa	L	1-2	Nicholl		39,144
13	Nov	5	(h)	Arsenal	L	1-2	Hill		53,055
14		12	(a)	Nottingham F	L	1-2	Pearson		30,183
15		19	(h)	Norwich C	W	1-0	Pearson		48,729
16		26	(a)	Q.P.R.	D	2-2	Hill 2		25,367
17	Dec	3	(h)	Wolves	W	3-1	McIlroy, J. Greenhoff, Pearson		48,874
18		10	(a)	West Ham U	L	1-2	McGrath		20,242
19		17	(h)	Nottingham F	L	0-4			54,374
20		26	(a)	Everton	W	6-2	Macari 2, Hill, J. Greenhoff, McIlroy, Ross (og)		48,335
21		27	(h)	Leicester C	W	3-1	J. Greenhoff, Coppell, Hill		57,396
22		31	(a)	Coventry C	L	0-3			24,706
23	Jan	2	(h)	Birmingham C	L	1-2	J. Greenhoff		53,501
24		14	(a)	Ipswich T	W	2-1	McIlroy, Pearson		23,321
25		21	(h)	Derby Co	W	4-0	Hill 2 (1 pen), Pearson, Buchan		57,115
26	Feb	8	(h)	Bristol C	D	1-1	Hill (pen)		43,457
27		11	(a)	Chelsea	D	2-2	McIlroy, Hill (pen)		32,849
28		25	(a)	Liverpool	L	1-3	McIlroy		49,094
29	Mar	1	(h)	Leeds U	L	0-1			49,101
30		4	(h)	Middlesbrough	D	0-0			46,332
31		11	(a)	Newcastle U	D	2-2	Jordan, Hill		25,825
32		15	(h)	Manchester C	D	2-2	Hill 2 (2 pens)		58,398
33		18	(h)	West Brom A	D	1-1	McQueen		46,329
34		25	(a)	Leicester C	W	3-2	Pearson, Hill, J. Greenhoff		20,299
35		28	(h)	Everton	L	1-2	Hill (pen)		55,277
36		29	(h)	Aston Villla	D	1-1	McIlroy		41,625
37	Apr	1	(a)	Arsenal	L	1-3	Jordan		40,829
38		8	(h)	Q.P.R.	W	3-1	Pearson 2 (1 pen), Grimes		42,677
39		15	(a)	Norwich C	W	3-1	Jordan, McIlroy, Coppell		19,778
40		22	(h)	West Ham U	W	3-0	Grimes (pen), McIlroy, Pearson		54,089
41		25	(a)	Bristol C	W	1-0	Pearson		26,035
42		29	(a)	Wolves	L	1-2	J. Greenhoff		24,774

FINAL LEAGUE POSITION: 10th in Division One

Appearances

Sub. Appearances

Goals

Stepney	Nicholl	Albiston	McIlroy	Greenhoff B	Buchan	Coppell	McCreery	Pearson	Macari	Hill	Grimes	McGrath	Forsyth	Houston	Greenhoff J	Rodgers	Roche	Ritchie	Jordan	McQueen	
1	2	3	4	5	6	7	8	9*	10	11	12										1
1	2	3	4	5	6	7	8	9	10	11											2
1	2	3	4*	5	6	9	8		10	11	12	7									3
1	5	3	4		6	7	8	9	10	11			2								4
1	5	3	4		6	7	8	9	10*	11		12	2								5
1	2	3	4	5	6*	7	8	9	10	11		12									6
1	2	3	4	5	6	7	8	9	10	11											7
1	2	3	4	5	6	7	8		10	11					9						8
1	2	3		5	6	9	4		10	11		7			8						9
1	2	3	4		6	9			10	11		7		5	8						10
1	5		4		6	7	8*	9	10	11		12	2			3					11
1	2	3	4		6	8	10	9		11*	12	7		5							12
1	2	3	4		6	8	10	9		11	12	7*		5							13
	2		4	5	6		8	10	9	11		7		3			1				14
	2		4*	5	6	7	12	9	10	11				3	8		1				15
	2			5	6	7		9	10*	11	4	12		3	8		1				16
	2	3	4	5		7		9		11	10*	12		6	8		1				17
	2	3		5		4		9		11	10	7		6	8		1				18
	2		4	5	6	7	9*	10		11	12			3	8		1				19
	2		4	5*	6	7		10		11	12			3	8		1	9			20
	2	3	4		6	7		10		11				5	8		1	9			21
	2		4	5	6	7		10		11	12			3*	8		1	9			22
	2	3	4	5	6	7		10		11					8		1	9			23
	2	3	4		6	7		9	10	11				5	8		1				24
	2	3	4		6	7		9	10	11				5	8		1				25
	2	3	4		6*	7		9	10	11				5	12		1		8		26
	2	3	4	6		7		9	10	11				5			1		8		27
	2	3	4			7		9	10	11*		12		6			1		8	5	28
	2	3	4	5		7		10		11				6	8		1		9		29
	2		4		6	7		10		11				3	8		1		9	5	30
	2		4		6	7		10		11				3	8		1		9	5	31
1	2	12	4		6	7		10		11				3	8				9*	5	32
1	2		4		6	7		9	10	11*		12		3	8					5	33
1	2		4		6	7		9	10	11				3	8					5	34
1	2	3	4		6	7		9	10	11					8					5	35
1			4	2	6	7	12	9	10					3	8*			11		5	36
1			4	2	6	7	12	9	10	11*				3				8		5	37
1			4	2	6	7	11	9			10			3				8		5	38
1		2	4	10	6	7	11*	9				12		3				8		5	39
1		2	4	11	6	7		9			10			3				8		5	40
	6	2	4	11		7		9			10			3			1	8		5	41
1	6	2	4	10*		7	12	9			11			3				8		5	42
23	37	27	39	31	28	42	13	30	32	36	7	9	3	31	22	1	19	4	14	14	
		1					4				6	9			1						
	2		9	1	1	4	1	10	8	17	2	1			6				3	1	

1978-79

#	Month	Date		Opponent	Result	Score	Scorers	Attendance
1	Aug	19	(h)	Birmingham C	W	1-0	Jordan	56,139
2		23	(a)	Leeds U	W	3-2	McQueen, McIlroy, Macari	36,845
3		26	(a)	Ipswich T	L	0-3		21,802
4	Sep	2	(h)	Everton	D	1-1	Buchan	53,982
5		9	(a)	Q.P.R.	D	1-1	J. Greenhoff	23,477
6		16	(h)	Nottingham F	D	1-1	J. Greenhoff	53,039
7		23	(a)	Arsenal	D	1-1	Coppell	45,393
8		30	(h)	Manchester C	W	1-0	Jordan	55,301
9	Oct	7	(h)	Middlesbrough	W	3-2	Macari 2, Jordan	45,402
10		14	(a)	Aston Villa	D	2-2	McIlroy, Macari	36,204
11		21	(h)	Bristol C	L	1-3	J. Greenhoff	47,211
12		28	(a)	Wolves	W	4-2	J. Greenhoff 2, B. Greenhoff, Jordan	23,141
13	Nov	4	(h)	Southampton	D	1-1	J. Greenhoff	46,259
14		11	(a)	Birmingham C	L	1-5	Jordan	23,550
15		18	(h)	Ipswich T	W	2-0	Coppell, J. Greenhoff	42,109
16		21	(a)	Everton	L	0-3		42,126
17		25	(a)	Chelsea	W	1-0	J. Greenhoff	28,163
18	Dec	9	(a)	Derby Co	W	3-1	Ritchie 2, J. Greenhoff	23,180
19		16	(h)	Tottenham H	W	2-0	Ritchie, McIlroy	52,026
20		22	(a)	Bolton W	L	0-3		32,390
21		26	(h)	Liverpool	L	0-3		54,910
22		30	(h)	West Brom A	L	3-5	B. Greenhoff, McQueen, McIlroy	45,091
23	Feb	3	(h)	Arsenal	L	0-2		45,460
24		10	(a)	Manchester C	W	3-0	Coppell 2, Ritchie	46,151
25		24	(h)	Aston Villa	D	1-1	J. Greenhoff (pen)	44,437
26		28	(h)	Q.P.R.	W	2-0	J. Greenhoff, Coppell	36,085
27	Mar	2	(a)	Bristol C	W	2-1	Ritchie, McQueen	24,583
28		20	(a)	Coventry C	L	3-4	Coppell 2, McIlroy	25,382
29		24	(h)	Leeds U	W	4-1	Ritchie 3, Thomas	51,191
30		27	(a)	Middlesbrough	D	2-2	McQueen, Coppell	20,138
31	Apr	7	(a)	Norwich C	D	2-2	McQueen, Macari	19,382
32		11	(h)	Bolton W	L	1-2	Buchan	49,617
33		14	(a)	Liverpool	L	0-2		46,608
34		16	(h)	Coventry C	D	0-0		43,035
35		18	(a)	Nottingham F	D	1-1	Jordan	33,074
36		21	(a)	Tottenham	D	1-1	McQueen	36,665
37		25	(h)	Norwich C	W	1-0	Macari	33,678
38		28	(h)	Derby Co	D	0-0		42,546
39		30	(a)	Southampton	D	1-1	Ritchie	21,616
40	May	5	(a)	West Brom A	L	0-1		27,960
41		7	(h)	Wolves	W	3-2	Ritchie, Coppell 2	39,402
42		16	(h)	Chelsea	D	1-1	Coppell	38,109

FINAL LEAGUE POSITION: 9th in Division One

Appearances

Sub. Appearances

Goals

Roche	Greenhoff B	Albiston	McIlroy	McQueen	Buchan	Coppell	Greenhoff J	Jordan	Macari	McCreery	McGrath	Nicholl	Grimes	Houston	Bailey	Sloan	Thomas	Ritchie	Paterson	Connell	Moran	#
1	2	3	4	5	6	7	8	9	10	11												1
1	2	3	4	5	6	7	8	9	10	11												2
1	2	3	4	5	6	7	8	9	10	11*	12											3
1	5	3	4		6	7	8	9	10	11*		2	12									4
1	2	3	4	5	6	7	8	9	10	11												5
1	2	3	4	5	6	7	8	9	10	11*			12									6
1	4	2	11	5	6	7	8	9	10					3								7
1	4	2	11	5	6	7	8	9	10					3								8
1		2	4	5	6	7	8*	9	10	11			12	3								9
1		2	4	5	6	7	8	9	10			11		3								10
1	12	2	4*	5	6	7	8	9	10			11		3								11
1	4		11	5*	6	7	8	9	10			2	12	3								12
1	5		4		6	7	8	9	10			2	11	3								13
1	5	12	11		6	7	8	9	10	4		2*		3								14
	4	2	11	5		7	8	9	12					3	1	10*						15
	4	2	11	5	6	7	8	9	12					3	1	10*						16
		2	4	5	6	7	8	9	10					3	1		11					17
		2	4	5	6	7	8		10					3*	1		11	9	12			18
		2	4	5	6	7	8		10					3	1		11	9				19
		2	4	5	6	7	8*		10			12			1		11	9	3			20
		2	4	5	6	7	8		10						1		11	9	3			21
		2	4	5	6	7	8*		10					3	1	12	11	9				22
		2	4	5	6	7	8*	9		4				3	1		11	12				23
	2	3	4	5	6	7	8		10						1		11	9				24
	2	3	4	5	6	7	8		10*			12			1		11	9				25
	2	3	4	5	6	7	8		10						1		11	9				26
		3	4	5	6	7	8					2	10		1		11	9				27
	10	3	4	5	6	7	8	9				2			1		11					28
	10	3	4	5	6	7	8*					2			1		11	9	12			29
	10	3	4	5	6	7	8	9				2			1		11					30
		2	4	5	6	7	8	9	10					3	1		11					31
		3	4	5	6	7		9	10			2			1		11	8				32
	5	3	4		6	7		9	10			2	12		1		11	8*				33
	10	3	4	5	6	7		9	12			2			1		11	8*				34
	10	3	4	5	6*	7		9	8			2	12		1		11					35
	6	3	4	5		7		9	10	8		2	12		1		11*					36
		3	4	5	6*	7		9	10	8		2	12		1		11					37
		3	4			7		9	10	2		5	12	6	1		11	8*				38
		2		5		7			10			11	3		1	4	9	8		6		39
	6	2	4	5		7		9	10			12	3		1		11*					40
	4*	3			6	7		9	10			2	12	5	1		11	8				41
		2	4	5		7	8	9	10*			6	12	3	1		11					42
14	32	32	40	36	37	42	33	30	31	14		19	5	21	28	3	25	16	1	2	1	
1	1							1	1	2	2	11	1		1			1	2			
2		5	6	2	11	11	6	6									1	10				

1979-80

#	Date		Venue	Opponent	Res	Score	Scorers	Att
1	Aug	18	(a)	Southampton	D	1-1	McQueen	21,768
2		22	(h)	West Brom A	W	2-0	Coppell, McQueen	53,377
3		25	(a)	Arsenal	D	0-0		44,380
4	Sep	1	(h)	Middlesbrough	W	2-1	Macari 2	51,015
5		8	(a)	Aston Villa	W	3-0	Coppell, Grimes, Thomas (pen)	34,859
6		15	(h)	Derby Co	W	1-0	Grimes	54,308
7		22	(a)	Wolves	L	1-3	Macari	35,503
8		29	(h)	Stoke C	W	4-0	McQueen 2, McIlroy, Wilkins	52,596
9	Oct	6	(h)	Brighton & H.A.	W	2-0	Coppell, Macari	52,641
10		10	(a)	West Brom A	L	0-2		27,713
11		13	(a)	Bristol C	D	1-1	Macari	28,305
12		20	(h)	Ipswich T	W	1-0	Grimes	50,826
13		27	(a)	Everton	D	0-0		37,708
14	Nov	3	(h)	Southampton	W	1-0	Macari	50,251
15		10	(a)	Manchester C	L	0-2		50,067
16		17	(h)	Crystal Palace	D	1-1	Jordan	52,800
17		24	(h)	Norwich C	W	5-0	Jordan 2, Coppell, Macari, Moran	46,540
18	Dec	1	(a)	Tottenham H	W	2-1	Coppell, Macari	51,389
19		8	(h)	Leeds U	D	1-1	Thomas	58,348
20		15	(a)	Coventry C	W	2-1	Macari, McQueen	25,541
21		22	(h)	Nottingham F	W	3-0	Jordan 2, McQueen	54,607
22		26	(a)	Liverpool	L	0-2		51,073
23		29	(h)	Arsenal	W	3-0	Jordan, McIlroy (pen), McQueen	54,295
24	Jan	12	(a)	Middlesbrough	D	1-1	Thomas	30,587
25	Feb	2	(a)	Derby Co	W	3-1	McIlroy, Thomas, B. Powell (og)	27,783
26		9	(h)	Wolves	L	0-1		51,568
27		16	(a)	Stoke C	D	1-1	Coppell	28,398
28		23	(h)	Bristol C	W	4-0	Jordan 2, McIlroy, Merrick (og)	43,329
29		27	(h)	Bolton W	W	2-0	Coppell, McQueen	47,546
30	Mar	1	(a)	Ipswich T	L	0-6		30,229
31		12	(h)	Everton	D	0-0		45,515
32		15	(a)	Brighton & H.A.	D	0-0		29,621
33		22	(h)	Manchester C	W	1-0	Thomas	56,387
34		29	(a)	Crystal Palace	W	2-0	Jordan, Thomas	33,056
35	Apr	2	(a)	Nottingham F	L	0-2		31,417
36		5	(h)	Liverpool	W	2-1	J. Greenhoff, Thomas	57,342
37		7	(a)	Bolton W	W	3-1	Coppell, McQueen, Thomas	31,902
38		12	(h)	Tottenham H	W	4-1	Ritchie 3, Wilkins	53,151
39		19	(a)	Norwich C	W	2-0	Jordan 2	23,274
40		23	(h)	Aston Villa	W	2-1	Jordan 2	45,207
41		26	(h)	Coventry C	W	2-1	McIlroy 2 (1 pen)	52,154
42	May	3	(a)	Leeds U	L	0-2		39,625

FINAL LEAGUE POSITION: 2nd in Division One

Appearances

Sub. Appearances

Goals

Bailey	Nicholl	Albiston	McIlroy	McQueen	Buchan	Coppell	Wilkins	Jordan	Macari	Thomas	Ritchie	Paterson	Grimes	Sloan	Houston	Moran	McGrath	Jovanovic	Greenhoff J	
1	2	3	4	5	6	7	8	9	10	11										1
1	2	3	4*	5	6	7	8	9	10	11	12									2
1	2	3	4	5	6	7*	8	9	10	11		12								3
1	2	3	4	5	6	7	8	9	10	11										4
1	2	3	4	5	6	7	8	9*	10	11			12							5
1	2	3	4	5	6	7	8		10		9		11							6
1	2	3	4	5	6	9	8		10*	11			7							7
1	2	3	4	5	6	9	8		10	11			7	12						8
1	2	3	4	5	6	9	8		10	11			7							9
1	2	3	4	5	6	9	8		10	11			7							10
1	2	3	4	5	6	9	8		10	11			7							11
1	2	3	4	5	6	9	8		10	11			7							12
1	2	3*	4	5	6	9	8		10	11			7	12						13
1	2		4		6	9	8		10	11			7		3	5				14
1	2		4		6	9	8		10	11			7		3	5				15
1	2		4		6	7	8	9	10	11*			12		3	5				16
1	2		4		6	7	8	9	10	11			3			5				17
1	2		4		6	7	8	9	10	11			3			5				18
1	2		4		6	7	8	9	10	11			3			5				19
1	2		4	5	6	7	8	9	10	11					3					20
1	2		4	5	6	7	8	9	10	11					3					21
1	2		4	5	6	7	8	9	10	11*			12		3					22
1	2		4	5	6	7	8	9	10	11					3					23
1	2		4	5	6	7	8	9	10	11*					3		12			24
1	2		4	5	6	7		9	10	11			12		3			8*		25
1	2		4	5	6	7	8*	9	10	11			12		3					26
1	2		4	5	6	7	8	9	10*		12		11		3					27
1	2		4	5*	6	7	8	9	10		12		11		3					28
1	2		4	5	6	7	8*	9	10				11	12	3					29
1	2*		4	5	6	7		9	10				11	8	3				12	30
1	2	3	4	5	6	7	8	9	10*				11					12		31
1	2	3	4	5	6	7	8	9	10				11							32
1	2	3	4	5	6	7	8	9	10	11*			12							33
1	2	3	4	5	6	7	8	9	10	11										34
1	2	3	4	5	6	7	8	9	10	11										35
1	2	3		5	6	7	8	9	10	11									4	36
1	2	3	4	5	6	7	8*	9		11	12		10							37
1	2	3	4	5	6	7	8	9		11	10									38
1	2	3	4		6	7	8	9		11	10					5				39
1	2	3	4		6	7		9	10	11						5			8	40
1	2	3	4		6	7		9	10	11			12			5			8*	41
1	2	3	4		6*	7		9	10	11	12								8	42
42	42	25	41	33	42	42	37	32	39	35	3		20	1	14	9		1	4	
											5	1	6	4			1	1	1	
			6	9		8	2	13	9	8	3		3		1				1	

1980-81

1	Aug	16	(h)	Middlesbrough	W	3-0	Macari, Grimes, Thomas	54,394
2		19	(a)	Wolves	L	0-1		31,955
3		23	(a)	Birmingham C	D	0-0		28,661
4		30	(h)	Sunderland	D	1-1	Jovanovic	51,498
5	Sep	6	(a)	Tottenham H	D	0-0		40,995
6		13	(h)	Leicester C	W	5-0	Coppell, Grimes, Jovanovic 2, Macari	43,229
7		20	(a)	Leeds	D	0-0		32,539
8		27	(h)	Manchester C	D	2-2	Coppell, Albiston	55,918
9	Oct	4	(a)	Nottingham F	W	2-1	Macari, Coppell	29,801
10		8	(h)	Aston Villa	D	3-3	McIlroy 2 (1 pen), Coppell	38,831
11		11	(h)	Arsenal	D	0-0		49,036
12		18	(a)	Ipswich T	D	1-1	McIlroy (pen)	28,572
13		22	(a)	Stoke C	W	2-1	Jordan, Macari	24,534
14		25	(h)	Everton	W	2-0	Jordan, Coppell	54,260
15	Nov	1	(a)	Crystal Palace	L	0-1		31,449
16		8	(h)	Coventry C	D	0-0		42,794
17		12	(h)	Wolves	D	0-0		37,959
18		15	(a)	Middlesbrough	D	1-1	Jordan	20,606
19		22	(a)	Brighton & H.A.	W	4-1	Jordan 2, McIlroy, Duxbury	23,293
20		29	(h)	Southampton	D	1-1	Jordan	46,840
21	Dec	6	(a)	Norwich C	D	2-2	Bond (og), Coppell	18,780
22		13	(h)	Stoke C	D	2-2	Macari, Jordan	39,568
23		20	(a)	Arsenal	L	1-2	Macari	33,730
24		26	(h)	Liverpool	D	0-0		57,049
25		27	(a)	West Brom A	L	1-3	Jovanovic	30,326
26	Jan	10	(h)	Brighton & H.A.	W	2-1	McQueen, Macari	42,208
27		28	(a)	Sunderland	L	0-2		31,910
28		31	(h)	Birmingham C	W	2-0	Jordan, Macari	39,081
29	Feb	7	(a)	Leicester C	L	0-1		26,085
30		17	(h)	Tottenham H	D	0-0		40,642
31		21	(a)	Manchester C	L	0-1		50,114
32		28	(h)	Leeds U	L	0-1		45,733
33	Mar	7	(a)	Southampton	L	0-1		22,698
34		14	(a)	Aston Villa	D	3-3	Jordan 2, McIlroy (pen)	42,182
35		18	(h)	Nottingham F	D	1-1	Burns (og)	38,205
36		21	(h)	Ipswich T	W	2-1	Thomas, Nicholl	46,685
37		28	(a)	Everton	W	1-0	Jordan	25,856
38	Apr	4	(h)	Crystal Palace	W	1-0	Duxbury	37,954
39		11	(a)	Coventry C	W	2-0	Jordan 2	20,201
40		14	(a)	Liverpool	W	1-0	McQueen	31,276
41		18	(h)	West Brom A	W	2-1	Jordan, Macari	44,442
42		25	(h)	Norwich C	W	1-0	Jordan	40,165

FINAL LEAGUE POSITION: 8th in Division One

Appearances

Sub. Appearances

Goals

Bailey	Nicholl	Albiston	McIlroy	Moran	Buchan	Coppell	Greenhoff J	Jordan	Macari	Thomas	Grimes	Roche	Ritchie	McGrath	Duxbury	Jovanovic	McGarvey	McQueen	Birtles	Sloan	Whelan	Wilkins	
1	2	3	4	5	6	7	8	9*	10	11	12												1
	2	3	4	5	6	9	8		10	11	7*	1	12										2
	2	3	4	5*	6		8		10	11		1	9	7	12								3
1	2	3	4		6	7	8		10	11			9			5							4
1	2	3	4		6	7	8		10	11			9*		12	5							5
1	2	3	4		6	9	8		10*	11	7					5	12						6
1	2	3	4		6	9	8		10*	11	7				12	5							7
1	2	3	4		6	9	8			11	7				10*	5		12					8
1	2	3	4	6		8		9	10	11					7	5							9
1	2	3	4	6		8	12	9	10*	11					7	5							10
1	2	3	4	6		8		9		11	7				10	5							11
1	2	3	4	6		7		9	10	11					8	5							12
1	2	3	4	6		7		9	10	11					12	5*			8				13
1	2	3	4	5		7		9	10	11					6				8				14
1	2	3	4	6		7		9	10	11						5			8				15
1	2	3	4	6		7		9	10	11						5*			8		12		16
1	2	3	4	5		7		9	10	11					6				8				17
1	2	3	4	5		7		9	10	11					6				8				18
1	2	3	4	6		7		9		11	12				10	5			8*				19
1		3	4	5*		7		9	10		11				6	2			8		12		20
1	2	3	4		6	7	8	9	10						11	5							21
1	2	3	4	6		7		9	10	11					8	5							22
1	2	3	4	6		7		9	10	11					8	5							23
1	2	3	4	6		7		9	10	11					8	5							4
1	2	3	4	6		7		9	10	11					8	5							25
1	2	3			6	7		9	10	11					12			5	8		4*		26
1	2	3			6	7		9	10	11					4			5	8				27
1	2	3	12		6	7		9	10	11*					4			5	8				28
1	2	3			6	7		9	10	11					4	5*			8		12		29
1	2	3	11	5	6	7			10						4			9	8				30
1	2	3	11	5	6	7			10						4*		12	9	8				31
1	2	3	11	5	6	7		9	10										8			4	32
1	2	3	11	5	6	7		9	10										8			4	33
1	2	3	11	5	6	7		9	10										8			4	34
1	2	3	11*	5	6	7		9	10						12				8			4	35
1	2	3		4	6	7		9		11					10			5	8				36
1	2*	3		4	6	7		9	12	11					10			5	8				37
1		3		4	6	7		9	10	11*					2			5	8			12	38
1		3		4	6	7		9	10						2			5	8			11	39
1		3		4	6	7		9	10						2			5	8			11	40
1		3		4	6	7		9	10						2			5	8			11	41
1		3		4	6	7		9	10						2			5	8			11	42
40	36	42	31	32	26	42	8	33	37	30	6	2	3	1	27	19		11	25			11	
			1			1			1		2		1		6		2			2	1	2	
	1	1	5			6		15	9	2	2				2	4		2					

1981-82

1	Aug	29	(a)	Coventry C	L	1-2	Macari		19,329
2		31	(h)	Nottingham F	D	0-0			51,496
3	Sep	5	(h)	Ipswich T	L	1-2	Stapleton		45,555
4		12	(a)	Aston Villa	D	1-1	Stapleton		37,661
5		19	(h)	Swansea C	W	1-0	Birtles		47,309
6		22	(a)	Middlesbrough	W	2-0	Stapleton, Birtles		19,895
7		26	(a)	Arsenal	D	0-0			39,795
8		30	(h)	Leeds	W	1-0	Stapleton		47,019
9	Oct	3	(h)	Wolves	W	5-0	Stapleton, McIlroy 3, Birtles		46,837
10		12	(a)	Manchester C	D	0-0			52,037
11		17	(h)	Birmingham C	D	1-1	Coppell		38,342
12		21	(h)	Middlesbrough	W	1-0	Moses		41,438
13		24	(a)	Liverpool	W	2-1	Moran, Albiston		45,928
14		31	(h)	Notts Co	W	2-1	Birtles, Moses		48,800
15	Nov	7	(a)	Sunderland	W	5-1	Moran, Robson, Stapleton 2, Birtles		27,070
16		21	(a)	Tottenham H	L	1-3	Birtles		35,534
17		28	(h)	Brighton & H.A.	W	2-0	Birtles, Stapleton		41,911
18	Dec	5	(a)	Southampton	L	2-3	Stapleton, Robson		24,404
19	Jan	6	(h)	Everton	D	1-1	Stapleton		40,451
20		23	(a)	Stoke C	W	3-0	Coppell, Stapleton (pen), Birtles		19,793
21		27	(h)	West Ham U	W	1-0	Macari		41,291
22		30	(a)	Swansea C	L	0-2			24,115
23	Feb	6	(h)	Aston Villa	W	4-1	Moran 2, Robson, Coppell		43,184
24		13	(a)	Wolves	W	1-0	Birtles		22,481
25		20	(h)	Arsenal	D	0-0			43,833
26		27	(h)	Manchester C	D	1-1	Moran		57,830
27	Mar	6	(a)	Birmingham C	W	1-0	Birtles		19,637
28		17	(h)	Coventry C	L	0-1			34,499
29		20	(a)	Notts Co	W	3-1	Coppell 2, Stapleton		17,048
30		27	(h)	Sunderland	D	0-0			40,776
31	Apr	3	(a)	Leeds U	D	0-0			30,953
32		7	(h)	Liverpool	L	0-1			48,371
33		10	(a)	Everton	D	3-3	Coppell 2, Grimes		29,306
34		12	(h)	West Brom A	W	1-0	Moran		38,717
35		17	(h)	Tottenham H	W	2-0	Coppell (pen), McGarvey		50,724
36		20	(a)	Ipswich T	L	1-2	Gidman		25,744
37		24	(a)	Brighton & H.A.	W	1-0	Wilkins		20,750
38	May	1	(h)	Southampton	W	1-0	McGarvey		40,038
39		5	(a)	Nottingham F	W	1-0	Stapleton		18,449
40		8	(a)	West Ham U	D	1-1	Moran		26,337
41		12	(a)	West Brom A	W	3-0	Robson, Birtles, Coppell		19,707
42		15	(h)	Stoke C	W	2-0	Robson, Whiteside		43,072

FINAL LEAGUE POSITION: 3rd in Division One

Appearances

Sub. Appearances

Goals

Bailey	Gidman	Albiston	Wilkins	McQueen	Buchan	Coppell	Birtles	Stapleton	Macari	McIlroy	Duxbury	Moses	Moran	Robson	Roche	Nicholl	McGarvey	Grimes	Whiteside	Davies	#
1	2	3	4	5	6	7	8	9	10	11											1
1	2	3	4	5	6	7	8	9	10	11											2
1	2	3	4	5	6	7	8	9	10	11*	12										3
1	2	3	4	5	6	7	8	9	10	11											4
1	2	3	4	5	6	7	8	9	10	11*			12								5
1	2	3	4	5	6*	7	8	9	10				12	11							6
1	2	3	4	5	6	7	8	9	10					11							7
1	2	3	4	5*	6	7	8	9		10			12	11							8
1	2	3	4		6	7	8	9		10			11	5							9
1	2	3	4		6	12	8*	9		10		11	5	7							10
1	2	3	4		6	11	8	9				10	5	7							11
1	2	3	4		6	11	8	9				5	10	7							12
1	2	3	4		6	11	8	9				10	5	7							13
1	2	3	4		6	11	8	9	12			5	10	7*							14
1	2*	3	4		6	11	8	9	12			10	5	7							15
		3	4		6*		8	9		11	2	10	5	7	1	12					16
	2	3	4		6		8	9		11		10	5	7	1						17
	2	3	4		6		8	9		11		10	5	7	1						18
1	2	3	4		6	11		9				10	5	7			8				19
1		3	4	5		11	8	9	10		2		6	7							20
1		3	4		6	11	8	9	10		2		5	7							21
1	12	3	4		6*	11	8	9	10		2		5	7							22
1	2	3	4		6	11	8*	9				10	5	7			12				23
1	2	3	4		6	11	8	9				10	5	7							24
1	2	3	4		6	11	8	9				10	5	7							25
1	2	3	4		6	11	8	9				10	5	7							26
1	2	3	4		6	11	8	9				10	5*	7			12				27
1	2	3	4		6	11	8	9	12			10	5	7*							28
1	2	3	4		6	11	8	9				10	5*	7			12				29
1	2	3	4	5	6	11	8*	9				10		7			12				30
1		3	4		6	11		9			2	10	5	7			8				31
1		3	4		6*	11		9			2	10	5	7			8	12			32
1	2	3	4			11		9		6		10*	5	7			8	12			33
1	2	3	4		6	11		9					5	7			8	10			34
1	2	3	4		6	11		9					5	7			8	10			35
1	2	3	4		6*		12	9		11			5	7			8	10			36
1	2	3	4		6			9		11*			5	7			8	10	12		37
1	2	3	4		6			9					5	7			8	10		11	38
1	2	3	4			11		9				6	5	7			8	10			39
1	2	3	4			11	8*	9				6	7	5			12	10			40
1	2	3	4		6	11	8	9					5	7				10			41
1	2	3	4		6	11	8*						5	7			12	10	9		42
39	36	42	42	21	27	35	32	41	10	12	19	20	30	32	3		10	9	1	1	
	1				1	1		1				5	1		1		6	2	1		
	1	1	1			9	11	13	2	3		2	7	5			2	1	1		

1982-83

1	Aug	28	(h)	Birmingham C	W	3-0	Moran, Stapleton, Coppell	48,673
2	Sep	1	(a)	Nottingham F	W	3-0	Wilkins, Whiteside, Robson	23,965
3		4	(a)	West Brom A	L	1-3	Robson	24,928
4		8	(h)	Everton	W	2-1	Whiteside, Robson	43,186
5		11	(h)	Ipswich T	W	3-1	Whiteside 2, Coppell	43,140
6		18	(a)	Southampton	W	1-0	Macari	21,700
7		25	(h)	Arsenal	D	0-0		43,198
8	Oct	2	(a)	Luton T	D	1-1	Grimes	17,009
9		9	(h)	Stoke C	W	1-0	Robson	43,132
10		16	(a)	Liverpool	D	0-0		40,853
11		23	(h)	Manchester C	D	2-2	Stapleton 2	57,334
12		30	(a)	West Ham U	L	1-3	Moran	31,684
13	Nov	6	(a)	Brighton & H.A.	L	0-1		18,379
14		13	(h)	Tottenham H	W	1-0	Muhren	47,869
15		20	(a)	Aston Villa	L	1-2	Stapleton	35,487
16		27	(h)	Norwich C	W	3-0	Muhren, Robson 2	34,579
17	Dec	4	(a)	Watford	W	1-0	Whiteside	25,669
18		11	(h)	Notts Co	W	4-0	Whiteside, Stapleton, Robson, Duxbury	33,618
19		18	(a)	Swansea C	D	0-0		15,748
20		27	(h)	Sunderland	D	0-0		47,783
21		28	(a)	Coventry C	L	0-3		18,945
22	Jan	1	(h)	Aston Villa	W	3-1	Stapleton 2, Coppell	41,545
23		3	(h)	West Brom A	D	0-0		39,123
24		15	(a)	Birmingham C	W	2-1	Whiteside, Robson	19,333
25		22	(h)	Nottingham F	W	2-0	Coppell (pen), Muhren	38,615
26	Feb	5	(a)	Ipswich T	D	1-1	Stapleton	23,804
27		26	(h)	Liverpool	D	1-1	Muhren	57,397
28	Mar	2	(a)	Stoke C	L	0-1		21,266
29		5	(a)	Manchester C	W	2-1	Stapleton 2	45,400
30		19	(h)	Brighton & H.A.	D	1-1	Albiston	36,264
31		22	(h)	West Ham U	W	2-1	Stapleton, McGarvey	30,227
32	Apr	2	(h)	Coventry C	W	3-0	Stapleton, Gillespie (og), Macari	36,814
33		4	(a)	Sunderland	D	0-0		31,486
34		9	(h)	Southampton	D	1-1	Robson	37,120
35		19	(a)	Everton	L	0-2		21,715
36		23	(h)	Watford	W	2-0	Cunningham, Grimes (pen)	43,048
37		30	(a)	Norwich C	D	1-1	Whiteside	22,233
38	May	2	(a)	Arsenal	L	0-3		23,602
39		7	(h)	Swansea C	W	2-1	Robson, Stapleton	35,724
40		9	(h)	Luton T	W	3-0	McGrath 2, Stapleton	24,213
41		11	(a)	Tottenham H	L	2-0		32,803
42		14	(a)	Notts Co	L	2-3	McGrath, Muhren	14,395

FINAL LEAGUE POSITION: 3rd in Division One

Appearances

Sub. Appearances

Goals

#	Bailey	Duxbury	Albiston	Wilkins	Moran	McQueen	Robson	Muhren	Stapleton	Whiteside	Coppell	Grimes	Macari	Buchan	Moses	McGrath P	McGarvey	Gidman	Wealands	Cunningham	Davies
1	1	2	3	4	5	6	7	8	9	10	11										
2	1	2	3	4	5	6	7	8	9	10	11										
3	1	2	3	4	5	6	7	8	9	10	11										
4	1	2	3	4	5	6	7	8	9	10	11										
5	1	2	3	4	5	6	7	8	9	10	11										
6	1	2	3	4		6	7		9	10	11*	8	12	5							
7	1	2	3	4	5	6	7		9	10		8	11								
8	1	2	3	4	5	6	7		9	10		8			11						
9	1	2	3	4	5	6	7		9	10		8			11						
10	1	2	3	4	5	6	7		9	10	11	8									
11	1	2	3	4	5	6	7	8*	9	10	11		12								
12	1	2	3		5		7	8	9	10	11	4		6							
13	1	2	3	5*		6	7	8	9	10	11	12			4						
14	1	2	3			6	7	8	9	10	11				4	5					
15	1	2	3		5	6	7	8	9	10*	11				4	12					
16	1	2	3		5	6	7	8	9	10	11				4						
17	1	2	3			6	7	8	9	10	11			5	4						
18	1	2	3		5	6	7*	8	9	10	11	12			4						
19	1	2	3		5	6	7	8	9	10	11				4						
20	1	2	3		5	6	7	8	9	10	11				4						
21	1	2	3	8	5	6	7		9			11			4		10				
22	1	2	3		5	6	7	8	9	10	11				4						
23	1	2	3		5	6	7	8	9	10	11				4						
24	1	2	3		5	6	7	8	9	10	11				4						
25	1	2	3		5	6	7	8	9	10	11				4						
26	1	2	3		5	6	7	8	9	10	11				4						
27	1	2	3	7	5*	6		8	9	10	11	12			4						
28	1	2	3	7		6		8	9	10	11				4	5					
29	1	2	3	7		6		8	9	10	11				4	5					
30	1	6	3	7*				8	9	10	11	12			4	5		2			
31	1	6	3	7				8	9*		11	12			4	5	10	2			
32		2	3	7		6		8	9	10*	11	12			4	5			1		
33		2	3	7		6		8	9	10*	11				4	5	12		1		
34	1	2	3	11		6	7	8	9	10					4	5					
35		2	3	8		6	7		9	10*	11				4	5			1	12	
36		2	3*	8		6	7		9	10	11				4	5			1	12	
37	1	2		8	5	6	7		9	10					3	4				11	
38	1	2		8	5	6			10						3	4		7		9	11
39	1	2		4*	5	6	7	8	9	10						3				11	12
40	1	2			5	6	7	8	9	10*					3	4	12			11	
41	1	2	3		5		7*	8	9	10	11			6	4		12				
42		6	3	7				8	9	10					4	5		2	1	11	
	37	42	38	26	29	37	33	32	41	39	29	15	2	3	29	14	3	3	5	3	2
													1	7			4			2	1
		1	1	1	2		10	5	14	8	4	2	2			3	1				1

1983-84

1	Aug	27	(h)	Q.P.R.	W	3-1	Muhren 2 (1 pen), Stapleton	48,742
2		29	(h)	Nottingham F	L	1-2	Moran	43,005
3	Sep	3	(a)	Stoke C	W	1-0	Muhren	23,704
4		6	(a)	Arsenal	W	3-2	Moran, Stapleton, Robson	42,703
5		10	(h)	Luton T	W	2-0	Muhren (pen), Albiston	41,013
6		17	(a)	Southampton	L	0-3		20,674
7		24	(h)	Liverpool	W	1-0	Stapleton	56,121
8	Oct	1	(a)	Norwich C	D	3-3	Whiteside 2, Stapleton	19,290
9		15	(h)	West Brom A	W	3-0	Graham, Whiteside, Albiston	42,221
10		22	(a)	Sunderland	W	1-0	Wilkins (pen)	26,826
11		29	(h)	Wolves	W	3-0	Stapleton 2, Robson	41,880
12	Nov	5	(h)	Aston Villa	L	1-2	Robson	45,077
13		12	(a)	Leicester C	D	1-1	Robson	24,409
14		19	(h)	Watford	W	4-1	Stapleton 3, Robson	43,111
15		27	(a)	West Ham U	D	1-1	Wilkins	23,355
16	Dec	3	(h)	Everton	L	0-1		43,664
17		10	(a)	Ipswich T	W	2-0	Graham, Crooks	19,779
18		16	(h)	Tottenham H	W	4-2	Graham 2, Moran 2	33,616
19		26	(a)	Coventry C	D	1-1	Muhren (pen)	21,553
20		27	(h)	Notts Co	D	3-3	Crooks, McQueen, Moran	41,544
21		31	(h)	Stoke C	W	1-0	Graham	40,164
22	Jan	2	(a)	Liverpool	D	1-1	Whiteside	44,622
23		13	(a)	Q.P.R.	D	1-1	Robson	16,308
24		21	(h)	Southampton	W	3-2	Robson, Stapleton, Muhren	40,371
25	Feb	4	(h)	Norwich C	D	0-0		36,851
26		7	(a)	Birmingham C	D	2-2	Whiteside, Hogg	19,957
27		12	(a)	Luton T	W	5-0	Robson 2, Whiteside 2, Stapleton	11,265
28		18	(a)	Wolves	D	1-1	Whiteside	20,676
29		25	(h)	Sunderland	W	2-1	Moran 2	40,615
30	Mar	3	(a)	Aston Villa	W	3-0	Moses, Whiteside, Robson	32,874
31		10	(h)	Leicester C	W	2-0	Moses, Hughes	39,473
32		17	(h)	Arsenal	W	4-0	Muhren 2 (1 pen), Stapleton, Robson	48,942
33		31	(a)	West Brom A	L	0-2		28,104
34	Apr	7	(h)	Birmingham C	W	1-0	Robson	39,896
35		14	(a)	Notts Co	L	0-1		13,911
36		17	(a)	Watford	D	0-0		20,764
37		21	(h)	Coventry C	W	4-1	Hughes 2, McGrath, Wilkins	38,524
38		28	(h)	West Ham U	D	0-0		44,124
39	May	5	(a)	Everton	D	1-1	Stapleton	28,802
40		7	(h)	Ipswich T	L	1-2	Hughes	44,257
41		12	(a)	Tottenham H	D	1-1	Whiteside	39,790
42		16	(a)	Nottingham F	L	0-2		23,651

FINAL LEAGUE POSITION: 4th in Division One

Appearances

Sub. Appearances

Goals

Bailey	Duxbury	Albiston	Wilkins	Moran	McQueen	Robson	Muhren	Stapleton	Whiteside	Graham	Macari	Gidman	Moses	McGrath	Crooks	Wealands	Hogg	Hughes	Davies	Blackmore	No.
1	2	3	4	5	6	7	8	9	10*	11	12										1
1	2*	3	4	5	6	7	8	9	10	11	12										2
1		3	4	5	6	7	8	9	10	11		2									3
1		3	4	5	6	7	8	9	10	11		2	12								4
1		3	4	5	6	7*	8	9	10	11*		2	12								5
1	2	3	4	5	6		8	9	10	11			7								6
1	2	3	4	5	6	7	8	9	10	11											7
1	2	3	4	5		7	8*	9	10	11			12	6							8
1	2	3	4	5	6	7	8	9	10	11											9
1	2	3	4	5*	6	7		9	10	11	12		8								10
1	5	3	4		6	7	8	9	10	11		2*	12								11
1	2	3	4	5	6	7		9	10*	11	12		8								12
1	2	3	4	5	6	7		9	10	11			8								13
1	5	3	4		6	7	8	9		11			2		10						14
1	5	3	4		6	7	8*	9	12	11			2		10						15
1	2	3	4	5	6	7		9		11			8		10						16
1	2	3	4	5	6	7		9		11			8		10						17
1	6	3	4	5		7	8	9*	10	11	12		2								18
	2	3	4	5	6		8	9		11			7		10	1					19
	2	3	4	5	6		8	9	12	11			7		10*	1					20
1	2	3	4	5	6		8	9	10	11			7								21
1	2	3	4	5*	6		8	9	10	11			7		12						22
1	2		4	5		7	8	9	10	11			3				6				23
1	2		4	5		7	8	9	10*	11			3				6	12			24
1	6	3	4	5		7	8	9	10	11			2								25
1	2	3	4	5		7		9	10	11			8				6				26
1	2	3	4	5		7*	8	9	10	12			11				6				27
1	2	3	4*	5		7	8	9	10	12			11				6				28
1	2	3	4	5*		7	8	9	10	12			11				6				29
1	2	3	4			7	8	9	10*	12			11	5			6				30
1	2	3	4	5		7	8	9					11				6	10			31
1	2	3	4	5		7	8	9	10*				11				6	12			32
1	2	3	4	5		7		9	10	8			11				6				33
1	2	3	4	5		7		9	10*	8			11				6	12			34
1	2	3	4	5				9	10				8	7			6	12	11*		35
1	2	3	4	5				9	10				8	7			6		11		36
1	2	3	4*	5				9	12	11			8	7			6	10			37
1	2	3	4	5				9	12	11			8	7			6	10			38
1	2	3	4	5		7		9	12				8				6	10	11*		39
1	2	3	4	5		7		9		11			8	6				10			40
1	2	3	4	5		7		9*	12	11			8	6				10			41
1	2	3	4	5		7		9	12	11*				6				10		8	42
40	39	40	42	38	20	33	26	42	30	33		4	31	9	6	2	16	7	3	1	
									7	4	5		4		1			4			
		2	3	7	1	12	8	13	10	5			2	1	2		1	4			

1984-85

1	Aug	25	(h)	Watford	D	1-1	Strachan (pen)	53,668
2		28	(a)	Southampton	D	0-0		22,183
3	Sep	1	(a)	Ipswich T	D	1-1	Hughes	20,434
4		5	(h)	Chelsea	D	1-1	Olsen	48,298
5		8	(h)	Newcastle U	W	5-0	Hughes, Moses, Olsen, Strachan 2 (1 pen)	54,915
6		15	(a)	Coventry C	W	3-0	Robson, Whiteside 2	18,482
7		22	(h)	Liverpool	D	1-1	Strachan (pen)	56,638
8		29	(a)	West Brom A	W	2-1	Robson, Strachan (pen)	26,401
9	Oct	6	(a)	Aston Villa	L	0-3		37,132
10		13	(h)	West Ham U	W	5-1	Brazil, Hughes, McQueen, Moses, Strachan	47,559
11		20	(h)	Tottenham H	W	1-0	Hughes	54,516
12		27	(a)	Everton	L	0-5		40,769
13	Nov	2	(h)	Arsenal	W	4-2	Hughes, Robson, Strachan 2	32,279
14		10	(a)	Leicester C	W	3-2	Brazil, Hughes, Strachan (pen)	23,840
15		17	(h)	Luton T	W	2-0	Whiteside 2	42,776
16		24	(a)	Sunderland	L	2-3	Hughes, Robson	25,405
17	Dec	1	(h)	Norwich C	W	2-0	Hughes, Robson	36,635
18		8	(a)	Nottingham F	L	2-3	Strachan 2 (1 pen)	25,902
19		15	(h)	Q.P.R.	W	3-0	Brazil, Duxbury, Gidman	36,134
20		22	(h)	Ipswich T	W	3-0	Gidman, Robson, Strachan (pen)	35,168
21		26	(a)	Stoke C	L	1-2	Stapleton	21,013
22		29	(a)	Chelsea	W	3-1	Hughes, Moses, Stapleton	42,197
23	Jan	1	(h)	Sheffield W	L	1-2	Hughes	47,638
24		12	(h)	Coventry C	L	0-1		35,992
25	Feb	2	(h)	West Brom A	W	2-0	Strachan 2	36,681
26		9	(a)	Newcastle U	D	1-1	Moran	31,798
27		23	(a)	Arsenal	W	1-0	Whiteside	48,612
28	Mar	2	(h)	Everton	D	1-1	Olsen	51,150
29		12	(a)	Tottenham H	W	2-1	Hughes, Whiteside	42,918
30		15	(a)	West Ham U	D	2-2	Robson, Stapleton	16,674
31		23	(h)	Aston Villa	W	4-0	Hughes 3, Whiteside	40,941
32		31	(a)	Liverpool	W	1-0	Stapleton	34,886
33	Apr	3	(h)	Leicester C	W	2-1	Robson, Stapleton	35,590
34		6	(h)	Stoke C	W	5-0	Hughes 2, Olsen 2, Whiteside	42,940
35		9	(a)	Sheffield W	L	0-1		39,380
36		21	(a)	Luton T	L	1-2	Whiteside	10,320
37		24	(h)	Southampton	D	0-0		31,291
38		27	(h)	Sunderland	D	2-2	Moran, Robson	38,979
39	May	4	(a)	Norwich C	W	1-0	Moran	16,006
40		6	(h)	Nottingham F	W	2-0	Gidman, Stapleton	43,334
41		11	(a)	Q.P.R.	W	3-1	Brazil 2, Strachan	20,483
42		13	(a)	Watford	L	1-5	Moran	20,047

FINAL LEAGUE POSITION: 4th in Division One

Appearances

Sub. Appearances

Goals

Bailey	Duxbury	Albiston	Moses	Moran	Hogg	Robson	Strachan	Hughes	Brazil	Olsen	Whiteside	Muhren	McQueen	Gidman	Stapleton	Garton	McGrath	Blackmore	Pears	
1	2	3	4	5	6	7	8	9	10*	11	12									1
1	2	3	4	5	6	7	8	9	10	11										2
1	2	3	4	5	6	7	8	9	10*	11	12									3
1	2	3	4	5	6	7	8	9		11	10									4
1	2	3	4	5	6	7	8	9		11	10									5
1	2	3	4	5	6	7	8	9		11	10									6
1	2	3	4	5*	6	7	8	9		11	10	12								7
1	2	3	4	5	6	7	8	9	10	11										8
1	2	3	4	5	6		7	9	10	11		8								9
1	2	3	4		6	7	8	9	10	11			5							10
1		3	4	5	6	7	8	9	10	11				2						11
1		3	4	5*	6	7	8	9	10	11				2	12					12
1		3	4	5	6	7	8	9		11				2	10					13
1		3	4		6	7	8	9	10	11	12			2			5			14
1	6	3	4			7*	8	9		11	10		5	2	12					15
1		3				7	8	9		11	10	12	5	2			6			16
1		3				7	8	9		11	10		5	2			6			17
1	2					7	8		10				5		9		6	3		18
1	6	3	4			7	8		10	11			5	2	9					19
1	6	3	4			7	8	9		11			5	2	10					20
1	6	3	4			7	8*	9	12	11			5	2	10					21
1	2	3	4			7	8*		10	11			5		9		6			22
1	2	3	4			7	8	9	10	11			5				6			23
	2	3	4			7*	8		10	11	12		5		9		6		1	24
		3	4	5	6		8	9		11	10			2			7		1	25
		3	4	5	6		8			11*	9			2	12		7		1	26
1	4	3	5*		6		8	9		11	12			2	10		7			27
1	4	3			6	7	9	8		11				2	10		5			28
1	4	3			6	7	9			11	8			2	10		5			29
1	4	3			6	7	9		12	11	8*			2	10		5			30
1		3			6	7	8	9		11	4			2	10		5			31
1		3			6	7	8	9		11	4			2	10		5			32
1		3			6	7	8	9		11	4			2	10		5			33
1	12	3			6	7*	8	9		11	4			2	10		5			34
	4*	3			6	7	8	9	12	11				2	10		5	1		35
1		3			6	7		9		11	4	8		2	10		5			36
1	12	3			6	7	8	9		11	4			2	10*		5			37
1	12	3			6	7	8	9	10	11	4			2*			5			38
1		3			6	7	8	9		11	4			2	10		5			39
1		3	5*		6		8		10	11	4	12		2	9		7			40
1	7	3			6*		8		10	11	4	12		2	9		5			41
1	7	3			6		8	9		11	4*	12		2	10		5			42
38	27	39	26	19	29	32	41	38	17	36	23	7	12	27	21	2	23	1	4	
	3			1			3		3	4	5			3						
	1		3	4		9	15	16	5	5	9			1	3		6			

39

1985-86

1	Aug	17	(h)	Aston Villa	W	4-0	Whiteside, Hughes 2, Olsen	49,743
2		20	(a)	Ipswich T	W	1-0	Robson	18,777
3		24	(a)	Arsenal	W	2-1	Hughes, McGrath	37,145
4		26	(h)	West Ham U	W	2-0	Hughes, Strachan	50,773
5		31	(a)	Nottingham F	W	3-1	Hughes, Barnes, Stapleton	26,274
6	Sep	4	(h)	Newcastle U	W	3-0	Stapleton 2, Hughes	51,102
7		7	(h)	Oxford U	W	3-0	Whiteside, Robson, Barnes	51,820
8		14	(a)	Manchester C	W	3-0	Robson (pen), Albiston, Duxbury	48,773
9		21	(a)	West Brom A	W	5-1	Brazil 2, Strachan, Blackmore, Stapleton	25,068
10		28	(h)	Southampton	W	1-0	Hughes	52,449
11	Oct	5	(a)	Luton T	D	1-1	Hughes	17,454
12		12	(h)	Q.P.R.	W	2-0	Hughes, Olsen	48,845
13		19	(h)	Liverpool	D	1-1	McGrath	54,492
14		26	(a)	Chelsea	W	2-1	Olsen, Hughes	42,485
15	Nov	2	(h)	Coventry C	W	2-0	Olsen 2	46,748
16		9	(a)	Sheffield W	L	0-1		48,105
17		16	(h)	Tottenham H	D	0-0		54,575
18		23	(a)	Leicester C	L	0-3		22,008
19		30	(h)	Watford	D	1-1	Brazil	42,181
20	Dec	7	(h)	Ipswich T	W	1-0	Stapleton	37,981
21		14	(a)	Aston Villa	W	3-1	Blackmore, Strachan, Hughes	27,626
22		21	(h)	Arsenal	L	0-1		44,386
23		26	(a)	Everton	L	1-3	Stapleton	42,551
24	Jan	1	(h)	Birmingham C	W	1-0	C. Gibson	43,095
25		11	(a)	Oxford U	W	3-1	Whiteside, Hughes, C. Gibson	13,280
26		18	(h)	Nottingham F	L	2-3	Olsen 2 (1 pen)	46,717
27	Feb	2	(a)	West Ham U	L	1-2	Robson	22,642
28		9	(a)	Liverpool	D	1-1	C. Gibson	35,064
29		22	(h)	West Brom A	W	3-0	Olsen 3 (2 pens)	45,193
30	Mar	1	(a)	Southampton	L	0-1		19,012
31		15	(a)	Q.P.R.	L	0-1		23,407
32		19	(h)	Luton T	W	2-0	Hughes, McGrath	33,668
33		22	(h)	Manchester C	D	2-2	C. Gibson, Strachan (pen)	51,274
34		29	(a)	Birmingham C	D	1-1	Robson	22,551
35		31	(h)	Everton	D	0-0		51,189
36	Apr	5	(a)	Coventry C	W	3-1	C. Gibson, Robson, Strachan	17,160
37		9	(h)	Chelsea	L	1-2	Olsen (pen)	45,355
38		13	(h)	Sheffield W	L	0-2		32,331
39		16	(a)	Newcastle U	W	4-2	Robson (pen), Hughes 2, Whiteside	31,840
40		19	(a)	Tottenham H	D	0-0		32,357
41		26	(h)	Leicester C	W	4-0	Stapleton, Hughes, Blackmore, Davenport (pen)	38,840
42	May	3	(a)	Watford	D	1-1	Hughes	18,414

FINAL LEAGUE POSITION: 4th in Division One

Appearances

Sub. Appearances

Goals

Bailey	Gidman	Albiston	Whiteside	McGrath	Hogg	Robson	Moses	Hughes	Stapleton	Olsen	Duxbury	Strachan	Brazil	Barnes	Moran	Blackmore	Garton	Gibson C	Dempsey	Turner	Wood	Gibson T	Sivebaek	Davenport	Higgins	
1	2	3	4	5	6	7	8*	9	10	11	12															1
1	2*	3	4	5	6	7		9	10	11	12	8														2
1		3	4	5	6	7		9	10	11	2	8														3
1		3	4	5	6	7		9	10	11	2	8														4
1		3	4	5	6	7		9	10		2	8*		12	11											5
1		3	4	5	6	7		9	10*		2	8		12	11											6
1		3	4	5	6	7		9	10*		2	8		12	11											7
1		3	4	5	6	7		9	10*		2	8		12	11											8
1		3	4	5	6	7		9			2	8*	10	12	11											9
1		3	4*	5		7	8	9	10		2			12	11	6										10
1		3	4	5		7	8	9	10		2				11	6										11
1		3	4	5		7		9	10	8	2				11	6										12
1		3	4	7	6		8*	9	10	11	2			12	5											13
1		3	4	7	6			9	10	8	2				11	5										14
1		3	4	7	6			9	10	8					11	5	2									15
1	2	3	4	5		7*		9	10	8				12	11	6										16
1	2	3	4	5				9	10	8		7			11	6										17
1	2	3*	4	7	6			9	10	11		8		12	5											18
1	2		4	7	6			9	10	11		8			5*			3								19
	2		4	5	6			9	10*	11		8		12				3	7	1						20
1	2		4	5	6	7		9	10*	11		8						3								21
1	2		4	5	6	7		9	10	11*		8		12				3								22
1	2		4	5	6	7		9	10	11*		8		12				3								23
	2	3	4	5*				9	10			8		12	6		7	11		1						24
1	2	3	4					9	10			8		7	5	6		11								25
1	2	3	4					9	10	7		8			5	6		11								26
1	2	3	4	5		7*		9	10			8		12		6		11								27
	2	3	4	5				9		11*		12			6			10		1		8	7			28
	2*	3		5				9	10	11		7			6		4	8		1			12			29
		3		5		7		9	10	11*	2	8			6			4		1			12			30
		3		5				9	7		2	8			6		4*	11		1			12	10		31
		3	4	5				9	12	11	2	8		6*				7		1				10		32
		3		5				9	12		2	8	11*					7		1				10	6	33
	2	3	4	5			7	9	12			8		11*						1				10	6	34
	2	3	4	5			7	9	12			8		11						1				10*	6	35
	2	3	4	5			7	9	12			8		11*						1				10	6	36
	2	3		5			7	9	12	11	4	8*								1				10	6	37
	2	3		5			7	9		11	4									1	12	8		10*	6	38
	2	3	4	5			7	9	10			11	6							1			8*	12		39
	2	3	4	5				9	10	12	7	11	6							1				8*		40
	2	3	4*	5				9	10	12	7	11	6							1				8		41
		3	4	5	6			9	10	12	7	11	2							1				8*		42
25	24	37	37	40	17	21	4	40	34	25	21	27	1	12	18	12	10	18	1	17		2	2	11	6	
								7	3	2	1	10	1	1				1				1	5	1		
		1	4	3		7		17	7	11	1	5		3	2		3							1		

41

1986-87

#							Scorers	Attendance
1	Aug	23	(a)	Arsenal	L	0-1		41,362
2		25	(h)	West Ham U	L	2-3	Stapleton, Davenport	43,306
3		30	(h)	Charlton Ath	L	0-1		37,544
4	Sep	6	(a)	Leicester C	D	1-1	Whiteside	16,785
5		13	(h)	Southampton	W	5-1	Olsen (pen), Davenport, Stapleton 2, Whiteside	40,135
6		16	(a)	Watford	L	0-1		21,650
7		21	(a)	Everton	L	1-3	Robson	25,843
8		28	(h)	Chelsea	L	0-1		33,340
9	Oct	4	(a)	Nottingham F	D	1-1	Robson	34,828
10		11	(h)	Sheffield W	W	3-1	Davenport 2 (1 pen), Whiteside	45,890
11		18	(h)	Luton T	W	1-0	Stapleton	39,927
12		26	(a)	Manchester C	D	1-1	Stapleton	32,440
13	Nov	1	(h)	Coventry C	D	1-1	Davenport	36,948
14		8	(a)	Oxford U	L	0-2		13,545
15		15	(a)	Norwich C	D	0-0		22,634
16		22	(h)	Q.P.R.	W	1-0	Sivebaek	42,235
17		29	(a)	Wimbledon	L	0-1		12,112
18	Dec	7	(h)	Tottenham H	D	3-3	Whiteside, Davenport 2 (1 pen)	35,957
19		13	(a)	Aston Villa	D	3-3	Davenport 2, Whiteside	29,205
20		20	(h)	Leicester C	W	2-0	C. Gibson, Stapleton	34,180
21		26	(a)	Liverpool	W	1-0	Whiteside	40,663
22		27	(h)	Norwich C	L	0-1		44,610
23	Jan	1	(h)	Newcastle U	W	4-1	P. Jackson (og), Whiteside, Stapleton, Olsen	43,334
24		3	(a)	Southampton	D	1-1	Olsen	20,409
25		24	(h)	Arsenal	W	2-0	Strachan, T. Gibson	51,367
26	Feb	7	(a)	Charlton Ath	D	0-0		15,482
27		14	(h)	Watford	W	3-1	McGrath, Davenport (pen), Strachan	35,763
28		21	(a)	Chelsea	D	1-1	Davenport (pen)	26,516
29		28	(h)	Everton	D	0-0		47,421
30	Mar	7	(h)	Manchester C	W	2-0	Reid (og), Robson	43,619
31		14	(a)	Luton T	L	1-2	Robson	12,509
32		21	(a)	Sheffield W	L	0-1		29,888
33		28	(h)	Nottingham F	W	2-0	McGrath, Robson	39,182
34	Apr	4	(h)	Oxford U	W	3-2	Davenport 2, Robson	32,443
35		14	(a)	West Ham U	D	0-0		23,486
36		18	(a)	Newcastle U	L	1-2	Strachan	32,706
37		20	(h)	Liverpool	W	1-0	Davenport	54,103
38		25	(a)	Q.P.R.	D	1-1	Strachan	17,414
39	May	2	(h)	Wimbledon	L	0-1		31,686
40		4	(a)	Tottenham H	L	0-4		36,692
41		6	(a)	Coventry C	D	1-1	Whiteside	23,407
42		9	(h)	Wimbledon	W	3-1	Blackmore, Duxbury, Robson	35,179

FINAL LEAGUE POSITION: 11th in Division One

Appearances

Sub. Appearances

Goals

	Turner	Duxbury	Albiston	Whiteside	McGrath	Moran	Strachan	Blackmore	Stapleton	Davenport	Gibson C	Olsen	Gibson T	Sivebaek	Hogg	Robson	Moses	Barnes	Walsh	O'Brien	Garton	Gill	Bailey	Wood	
1	1	2	3	4	5	6	7	8	9	10	11*	12													1
2	1	2	3	4	5	6	7	8	9	10	11*	12													2
3	1	2	3	4*	5	6	7	8	9	10			11	12											3
4	1	8	3	4	5		7		9	12			11	10*	2	6									4
5	1		3	4	5	6	8*		9	10			11	12	2		7								5
6	1		3		5	6		8	9	10			11		2		7	4							6
7	1		3	4*	5	6		8	9	10			12		2		7	11							7
8	1		3	4	5	6		8	9	10			12		2		7	11*							8
9	1		3	4	5	6		8	9	10			11		2		7								9
10	1		3	4	5			8	9	10					2	6	7		11						10
11	1		3	4	5		8*		9	10		12			2	6	7		11						11
12	1		3	4	5				9	10					2	6	7	8	11						12
13	1		3	4	5			8	9	10		11			2	6	7*	12							13
14	1	2	3		5*	4		7	9	10		12				6		8	11						14
15	1	3		5	12		8		9	10		7	2*	6		4			11						15
16	1	3		5			12	8	9	10		7	2	6		4			11*						16
17	1	3		5	6		8		9	10		7	2			12	4		11*						17
18	1	3		9	5*		6	8		12	10		11		2		7	4							18
19		3		9	5		8			12	10*	11			2	6	7	4	1						19
20				9	5	8			12	10	3	11			2	6	7		1	4*					20
21		6		4		5	8		9	10	3	11			2		7		1						21
22		6		4			8		9	10	3	11			2		7*		1	12	5				22
23	1	7		9*		6		8	12	10	3	11			2					4	5				23
24	1	2			6	8			9	12	3	11	10							4	5	7*			24
25	1	3*		4	12	6	8	7	9			11	10		2						5				25
26	1	4			6	8			9	12	3	11	10*		2		7				5				26
27	1	4		5		6	8		12	9	3	11	10				7			2*					27
28		2		4	5	6	8		12	9	3	11*	10				7					1			28
29		2		4	5	6	11		9*		3		10		8	7		12				1			29
30		4		9	5	6	8*			12	3		10	2		7		11				1			30
31		4		9	5	6	8			12	3*		10	2		7		11				1			31
32		3		9	5	6	8			10	11		12			7				4	2*	1			32
33		6	12	10	5				9		3				2	7	8		1	4			11*		33
34		6	12		5				9	11	3				2	7	8		1	4			10*		34
35		2	12		5	6	8		9	11	3		10			7*	4		1						35
36		2	10		5	6	8		12	11	3		9*				4		1	7					36
37		7	3*	10	5	6	8		12	9	11			2			4		1						37
38		2	3	9	5	6	8			10	11		12			7	4*		1						38
39		2	3		5	6	8		12	9	11	10				7	4*		1						39
40		4	10		5	6	8	12			3	11	9	2*		7			1						40
41		4	3	9	5	6	8*	12		10	11					7			1		2				41
42		4	3	9*	5	6		8		10	11	12				7			1		2				42
	23	32	19	31	34	32	33	10	25	34	24	22	12	27	11	29	17	7	14	9	9	1	5	2	
		3		1	1	1	2	9	5		6	4	1		1	1			3						
		1		8	2		4	1	7	14	1	3	1	1		7									

43

1987-88

#	Month	Date		Opponent	Res	Score	Scorers	Att
1	Aug	15	(a)	Southampton	D	2-2	Whiteside 2	21,214
2		19	(h)	Arsenal	D	0-0		42,890
3		22	(h)	Watford	W	2-0	McGrath, McClair	38,582
4		29	(a)	Charlton Ath	W	3-1	McClair, Robson, McGrath	14,046
5		31	(h)	Chelsea	W	3-1	McClair, Strachan, Whiteside	46,478
6	Sep	5	(a)	Coventry C	D	0-0		27,125
7		12	(h)	Newcastle U	D	2-2	Olsen, McClair (pen)	45,137
8		19	(a)	Everton	L	1-2	Whiteside	38,439
9		26	(h)	Tottenham H	W	1-0	McClair (pen)	47,601
10	Oct	3	(a)	Luton T	D	1-1	McClair	9,137
11		10	(a)	Sheffield W	W	4-2	Robson, McClair 2, Blackmore	32,779
12		17	(h)	Norwich C	W	2-1	Davenport, Robson	39,345
13		25	(a)	West Ham U	D	1-1	Gibson	19,863
14		31	(h)	Nottingham F	D	2-2	Robson, Whiteside	44,669
15	Nov	15	(h)	Liverpool	D	1-1	Whiteside	47,106
16		21	(a)	Wimbledon	L	1-2	Blackmore	11,532
17	Dec	5	(a)	Q.P.R.	W	2-0	Davenport, Robson	20,632
18		12	(h)	Oxford U	W	3-1	Strachan 2, Olsen	34,709
19		19	(a)	Portsmouth	W	2-1	Robson, McClair	22,207
20		26	(a)	Newcastle U	L	0-1		26,461
21		28	(h)	Everton	W	2-1	McClair 2 (1 pen)	47,024
22	Jan	1	(h)	Charlton Ath	D	0-0		37,257
23		2	(a)	Watford	W	1-0	McClair	18,038
24		16	(h)	Southampton	L	0-2		35,716
25		24	(a)	Arsenal	W	2-1	Strachan, McClair	29,392
26	Feb	6	(h)	Coventry C	W	1-0	O'Brien	37,144
27		10	(a)	Derby Co	W	2-1	Whiteside, Strachan	20,016
28		13	(a)	Chelsea	W	2-1	Bruce, O'Brien	25,014
29		23	(a)	Tottenham H	D	1-1	McClair	25,731
30	Mar	5	(a)	Norwich C	L	0-1		19,129
31		12	(h)	Sheffield W	W	4-1	Blackmore, McClair 2, Davenport	33,318
32		19	(a)	Nottingham F	D	0-0		27,598
33		26	(h)	West Ham U	W	3-1	Strachan, Anderson, Robson	37,269
34	Apr	2	(h)	Derby Co	W	4-1	McClair 3, Gibson	40,146
35		4	(a)	Liverpool	D	3-3	Robson 2, Strachan	43,497
36		12	(h)	Luton T	W	3-0	McClair, Robson, Davenport	28,830
37		30	(h)	Q.P.R.	W	2-1	Bruce, Parker (og)	35,733
38	May	2	(a)	Oxford U	W	2-0	Anderson, Strachan	8,966
39		7	(h)	Portsmouth	W	4-1	McClair 2 (1 pen), Davenport, Robson	35,105
40		9	(h)	Wimbledon	W	2-1	McClair 2 (1 pen)	28,040

FINAL LEAGUE POSITION: 2nd in Division One

Appearances

Sub. Appearances

Goals

Player appearances / goals grid (Manchester United, 1987–88 season).

Walsh	Anderson	Duxbury	Moses	McGrath	Moran	Robson	Strachan	McClair	Whiteside	Olsen	Albiston	Davenport	Gibson	Hogg	Garton	Blackmore	O'Brien	Graham	Turner	Bruce	Martin	Match
1	2	3	4*	5	6	7	8	9	10	11†	12	14										1
1	2	3	4	5	6	7	8	9	10	11												2
1	2	3	4	5	6	7	8*	9	10	11†	14	12										3
1	2	3	4	5	6	7	8*	9	10	11†		14	12									4
1	2	7	4	5	6		8	9	10	11	3*	12										5
1	2	7	4	5	6		8	9	10	11†	3*	14	12									6
1	2	3	4	5	6	7	8	9	10	11*		12										7
1	2	3	4	5		7	8†	9	10	11		14		6*	12							8
1	2*	6		5		7	8†	9	10	11		14	3		4	12						9
1		6		5		7	8	9	10	11			3	4	2*	12						10
1			4	5	6*	7	8†	9	10	11		14	3		2	12						11
1			4	5	12	7		9	10	11		8	3	2*	6†	14						12
1	2		4	5	6	7	8*	9		11		10	3			12						13
1	2		4		6	7	12	9	10*	11		8	3	5								14
1	2		4		6*	7	8	9	10	11		12	3	5								15
1	2	3*	4		6	7		9	10	11		12	5				14	8†				16
	2	4		5		7	8	9		11	3	10				6			1			17
	2	4		5		7*	8	9	10	11		12	6			3			1			18
	2	6		5		7	8	9	10	11*		12	3						1	4		19
12	2	6†		5		7	8	9	10			14	11			3*			1	4		20
	2	6	12	5		7	8*	9	10†	11		14	3						1	4		21
	2	5			6*	7	8	9		11†		10	3			14	12		1	4		22
	2	6		5†		7	8	9	10		3*	12	11			14			1	4		23
	2	8	6	5†		7	12	9		11		10	3*			14			1	4		24
	2	3				7	8	9	10	11			6			5*	12		1	4		25
	2	3				7	8	9	10	11		12	6			5*			1	4		26
	2	3*				7	8	9	10	11†	12	14	6			5			1	4		27
	2					7		9	10		3	8	11*	6	12	5			1	4		28
	2†	3	12					9	10	14		7	11	6*		5	8		1	4		29
		3*			6	7	8	9	12	10		11			2	5			1	4		30
		5				7	8	9	11*	10	3		6		2	12			1	4		31
	2	5	14			7	8	9	10	11*		12	3	6†					1	4		32
	2	6		5		7	8*	9	12	10		11	3						1	4		33
	2	6		5†		7	8	9	12	10*		11	4	3		14			1			34
	2	6*		5		7	8	9	14	12		10	11			3†			1	4		35
	2	6		5		7	8	9	12	10		11*	3						1	4		36
	2	6		5		7	8	9	11	10			3*			12			1	4		37
	2*	6		5		7	8	9	11	10			3			12			1	4		38
	2†	6		5*		7	8	9	11	10			3			12	14		1	4		39
	2	6*		5		7	8	9	10	11			3						1	4	12	40
16	30	39	16	21	20	36	33	40	26	30	5	21	26	9	5	15	6	1	24	21		
	1		1	1	1		3		1	7	6	13	3	1	1	7	11			1		
	2		2		11	8	24	7	2		5	2		3	2			2					

45

1988-89

								Attendance
1	Aug	27	(h)	Q.P.R.	D	0-0		26,377
2	Sep	3	(a)	Liverpool	L	0-1		42,026
3		10	(h)	Middlesbrough	W	1-0	Robson	40,422
4		17	(a)	Luton T	W	2-0	Davenport, Robson	11,010
5		24	(h)	West Ham U	W	2-0	Davenport, Hughes	29,941
6	Oct	1	(a)	Tottenham H	D	2-2	Hughes, McClair	29,318
7		22	(a)	Wimbledon	D	1-1	Hughes	12,143
8		26	(h)	Norwich C	L	1-2	Hughes	36,998
9		30	(a)	Everton	D	1-1	Hughes	27,005
10	Nov	5	(h)	Aston Villa	D	1-1	Bruce	44,804
11		12	(a)	Derby Co	D	2-2	Hughes, McClair	24,080
12		19	(h)	Southampton	D	2-2	Robson, Hughes	37,277
13		23	(h)	Sheffield W	D	1-1	Hughes	30,867
14		27	(a)	Newcastle U	D	0-0		20,350
15	Dec	3	(h)	Charlton Ath	W	3-0	Milne, McClair, Hughes	31,173
16		10	(a)	Coventry C	L	0-1		19,936
17		17	(a)	Arsenal	L	1-2	Hughes	37,422
18		26	(h)	Nottingham F	W	2-0	Milne, Hughes	39,582
19	Jan	1	(h)	Liverpool	W	3-1	McClair, Hughes, Beardsmore	44,745
20		2	(a)	Middlesbrough	L	0-1		24,411
21		14	(h)	Millwall	W	3-0	Blackmore, Gill, Hughes	40,931
22		21	(a)	West Ham U	W	3-1	Strachan, Martin, McClair	29,822
23	Feb	5	(h)	Tottenham H	W	1-0	McClair	41,423
24		11	(a)	Sheffield W	W	2-0	McClair 2	34,820
25		25	(a)	Norwich C	L	1-2	McGrath	23,155
26	Mar	12	(a)	Aston Villa	D	0-0		28,332
27		25	(h)	Luton T	W	2-0	Milne, Blackmore	36,335
28		27	(a)	Nottingham F	L	0-2		30,092
29	Apr	2	(h)	Arsenal	D	1-1	Adams (og)	37,977
30		8	(a)	Millwall	D	0-0		17,523
31		15	(h)	Derby Co	L	0-2		34,145
32		22	(a)	Charlton Ath	L	0-1		12,056
33		29	(h)	Coventry C	L	0-1		29,799
34	May	2	(h)	Wimbledon	W	1-0	McClair	23,368
35		6	(a)	Southampton	L	1-2	Beardsmore	17,021
36		8	(a)	Q.P.R.	L	2-3	Bruce, Blackmore	10,017
37		10	(h)	Everton	L	1-2	Hughes	26,722
38		13	(h)	Newcastle U	W	2-0	McClair, Robson	30,379

FINAL LEAGUE POSITION: 11th in Division One

Appearances

Sub. Appearances

Goals

Leighton	Blackmore	Martin	Bruce	McGrath	McClair	Robson	Strachan	Davenport	Hughes	Olsen	O'Brien	Anderson	Duxbury	Garton	Sharpe	Beardsmore	Robins	Donaghy	Gibson	Milne	Gill	Wilson	Maiorana	Whiteside	Brazil	
1	2	3	4	5	6	7	8	9*	10	11	12															1
1	3		4	5*	9	7	8†	14	10	11		2	6	12												2
1	3		4	5	9	7		8	10	11			6	2												3
1	3		4	5	9	7		8	10	11			6	2												4
1	2		4		9	7	8	11	10	12			6	5†	3*	14										5
1			4	5	9	7	8	11*	10	12		14	6	2†	3											6
1	2		4		9	7	8*	11†	10				6	5	3	12	14									7
1	2		4		9	7	8	11*	10	12			6	5	3											8
1	3		4		9	7	8*		10	11	14		5	2				6†	12							9
1	2		4		9	7	8		10	11	5		12					6	3*							10
1	3		4		9	7	8		10	12			5*	2	11			6								11
1	3		4		9	7	8		10					2	11*			6		5	12					12
1	3†		4		9	7	8*		10					2	11			6		5	12	14				13
1	3	12	4		9	7			10					2	11†		14	6		8*	5					14
1	5	3	4		9	7	8		10					2				6		11						15
1	5	3	4		9	7	8		10					2*	11			6		14	12†					16
1	5*	2†	4		9	7	8		10						3	14		6		11	12					17
1		2	4		9	7	8		10						3	5		6		11						18
1		2*	4	12	9	7	8†		10						3	5	14	6		11						19
1			4	5	9	7			10						3	8*	14	6		11	2†	12				20
1	8	2	4		9				10						3	5*		6		11†	7	12	14			21
1	5	3	4		9	7	8*		10						12			6		11	2					22
1	5	2	4	12	9	7	8†		10						3*	14		6		11						23
1	5	3	4	2	9	7	8		10*							12		6		11						24
1	2†	12	4	5	9	7	8		10						3	14		6		11*						25
1	12	3†	4	5	9	7	8		10						11	2*		6		14						26
1	3	2	4	5	9	7			10						8*			6		11		12				27
1	3	12	4	5*	9	7			10			2			8			6		11†	14					28
1	14	12	4	5	9	7			10			2			8†		3				11*	6				29
1		11	4	5*	9	7			10			2			8		3				12	6				30
1		3	4	5	9				10			2†	12		8*	7	6				14	11				31
1			4	5	9	7			10				2		8	12	3	11*				6				32
1		11*	4	5	9	7			10				2		8	12	3					6				33
1		11	4	5	9	7			10				2		8		3				12	6*				34
1		11*	4	5	9	7†			10				2		12	8	3	14				6				35
1	5	11	4		9				10				2		3*	8	6	7								36
1	5*	11	4		9				10				2†		3	8	12	6	7					14		37
1	5†	3	4		9	7			10				2		14	8	12	6	11*							38
38	26	20	38	18	38	34	21	7	38	6	1	5	16	13	19	17	1	30	1	19	4		2	6		
	2	4		2				1			4	2	1	2	1	3	6	9		1	3	5	4	4	1	
	3	1	2	1	10	4	1	2	14							2				3	1					

47

1989-90

1	Aug	19	(h)	Arsenal	W	4-1	Bruce, Hughes, Webb, McClair	47,245
2		22	(a)	Crystal Palace	D	1-1	Robson	22,423
3		26	(a)	Derby Co	L	0-2		22,175
4		30	(h)	Norwich C	L	0-2		39,610
5	Sep	9	(a)	Everton	L	2-3	McClair, Beardsmore	37,916
6		16	(h)	Millwall	W	5-1	Hughes 3, Robson, Sharpe	42,746
7		23	(a)	Manchester C	L	1-5	Hughes	43,246
8	Oct	14	(h)	Sheffield W	D	0-0		41,492
9		21	(a)	Coventry C	W	4-1	Bruce, Hughes 2, Phelan	19,605
10		28	(h)	Southampton	W	2-1	McClair 2	37,122
11	Nov	4	(a)	Charlton Ath	L	0-2		16,065
12		12	(h)	Nottingham F	W	1-0	Pallister	34,182
13		18	(a)	Luton T	W	3-1	Wallace, Blackmore, Hughes	11,141
14		25	(h)	Chelsea	D	0-0		47,106
15	Dec	3	(a)	Arsenal	L	0-1		34,484
16		9	(h)	Crystal Palace	L	1-2	Beardsmore	33,514
17		16	(h)	Tottenham H	L	0-1		36,230
18		23	(a)	Liverpool	D	0-0		37,426
19		26	(a)	Aston Villa	L	0-3		41,247
20		30	(a)	Wimbledon	D	2-2	Hughes, Robins	9,622
21	Jan	1	(h)	Q.P.R.	D	0-0		34,824
22		13	(h)	Derby Co	L	1-2	Pallister	38,985
23		21	(a)	Norwich C	L	0-2		17,370
24	Feb	3	(h)	Manchester C	D	1-1	Blackmore	40,274
25		10	(a)	Millwall	W	2-1	Wallace, Hughes	15,491
26		24	(a)	Chelsea	L	0-1		29,979
27	Mar	3	(h)	Luton T	W	4-1	McClair, Hughes, Wallace, Robins	35,327
28		14	(h)	Everton	D	0-0		37,398
29		18	(h)	Liverpool	L	1-2	Whelan (og)	46,629
30		21	(a)	Sheffield W	L	0-1		33,260
31		24	(a)	Southampton	W	2-0	Gibson, Robins	20,510
32		31	(h)	Coventry C	W	3-0	Hughes 2, Robins	39,172
33	Apr	14	(a)	Q.P.R.	W	2-1	Robins, Webb	18,997
34		17	(h)	Aston Villa	W	2-0	Robins 2	44,080
35		21	(a)	Tottenham H	L	1-2	Bruce (pen)	33,317
36		30	(h)	Wimbledon	D	0-0		29,281
37	May	2	(a)	Nottingham F	L	0-4		21,186
38		5	(h)	Charlton Ath	W	1-0	Pallister	35,389

FINAL LEAGUE POSITION: 13th in Division One

Appearances

Sub. Appearances

Goals

Leighton	Duxbury	Blackmore	Bruce	Phelan	Donaghy	Robson	Webb	McClair	Hughes	Sharpe	Martin	Graham	Pallister	Robins	Anderson	Beardsmore	Ince	Wallace	Maiorana	Milne	Brazil	Gibson	Sealey	Bosnich	No.
1	2	3	4	5	6	7	8	9	10	11*	12														
1	2	3	4	5	6	7	8	9	10	11															1
1	2	6	4	5		7	8	9	10	11	3*	12													2
1	2	3†	4	5		7*	8	9	10	11	12		6	14											3
1	2*	8	4	5	7			9	10	11	3†		6		12	14									4
1	12		4†	5	3	7		9	10	11			6		2	14	8*								5
1	4			5	3			9	10	12			6		2	7*	8	11							6
1	2*		4	5	3	7		9	10	14	12		6				8	11†							7
1	12		4	5	2	7		9	10	11†	3		6				8*	14							8
1		12	4	5	2	7		9	10	11	3		6				8*								9
1		12	4	5	2†	7		9	10	11*	3		6				8	14							10
1		2	4	5		7		9	10	12	3		6				8	11*							11
1		2	4	5		7		9	10		3		6				8	11							12
1	12	2	4	5		7		9	10		3*		6			14	8	11†							13
1		2*	4	5		7		9	10		3		6			12	8	11							14
1		14	4	5†		7		9	12	10*	3		6			2	8	11							15
1		14	4*	5		7		9	10		3		6	12	2†		8	11							16
1		2	4	5		7		9	10	12	3		6				8	11*							17
1	12	7†	4	5				9	10	11	3*		6	14	2		8								18
1	7		4	5				9	10	12	3		6	11	2		8*								19
1	12	8†	4	5				9	10	7*	3		6	11	2	14									20
1	12	8*	4	5				9	10		3		6	11	2	7†									21
1		14	4	5†				9	10				6	7	2	12	8*	11	14						22
1	8	7		5	4*			9	10		3		6	14	2	12		11†							23
1	8	7†		5				9	10		3		6	14	2*	4		11							24
1	7*		4	5	14			9	10		3		6		2†	12	8	11		12					25
1			4	5				9	10		3		6	7	2	12	8	11*							26
1	2	14	4	5				9	10*		3		6	7†		12	8	11							27
1	12	7	4	5				9	10		3		6		2*	14	8	11†							28
1		11*	4	5	2			9	10		3		6	7†		12	14								29
1			4	5	2		12	9	10†		3		6	14			8	11†			8				30
1			4	5	2		12	9	10†		3		6	14			8	11†			7*				31
1			4	5	2*	7		9	10	12			6	14			8	11†			3				32
			4*	5		7	8	9	10†		3		6	14	2			11			12	1			33
		14	4	5		7	8†	9	10				6	4	2	12		11*			3†	1			34
		14	4	5					10		3		6	9*	2	7	8	12			11†		1		35
1	2	3	4	5			8	9					6	10		7		11							36
1			4	5		7	8	9	10		3		6		2			11							37
1			4	5		7	8	9	10		3		6		2			11							38
35	12	19	34	38	13	20	10	37	36	13	28		35	10	14	8	25	23			5	2	1		
	7	9		1		1		1	5	4	1		7	2	13	1		3	1	1	1	1	1		
		2	3	1		2	2	5	13	1			3	7	2			3			1				

1990-91

1	Aug	25	(h)	Coventry C	W	2-0	Bruce, Webb		46,715
2		28	(a)	Leeds U	D	0-0			29,172
3	Sep	1	(a)	Sunderland	L	1-2	McClair		26,105
4		4	(a)	Luton T	W	1-0	Robins		12,576
5		8	(h)	Q.P.R.	W	3-1	McClair, Robins 2		43,427
6		16	(a)	Liverpool	L	0-4			35,726
7		22	(h)	Southampton	W	3-2	McClair, Blackmore, Hughes		41,228
8		29	(h)	Nottingham F	L	0-1			46,766
9	Oct	20	(h)	Arsenal	L	0-1			47,232
10		27	(a)	Manchester C	D	3-3	Hughes, McClair 2		36,427
11	Nov	3	(h)	Crystal Palace	W	2-0	Webb, Wallace		45,724
12		10	(a)	Derby Co	D	0-0			21,115
13		17	(h)	Sheffield U	W	2-0	Bruce, Hughes		45,903
14		25	(h)	Chelsea	L	2-3	Wallace, Hughes		37,836
15	Dec	1	(a)	Everton	W	1-0	Sharpe		32,400
16		8	(h)	Leeds U	D	1-1	Webb		40,927
17		15	(a)	Coventry C	D	2-2	Hughes, Wallace		17,106
18		22	(a)	Wimbledon	W	3-1	Bruce 2 (2 pens), Hughes		9,744
19		26	(h)	Norwich C	W	3-0	Hughes, McClair 2		39,801
20		29	(h)	Aston Villa	D	1-1	Bruce (pen)		47,485
21	Jan	1	(a)	Tottenham H	W	2-1	Bruce (pen), McClair		29,399
22		12	(h)	Sunderland	W	3-0	Hughes 2, McClair		45,934
23		19	(a)	Q.P.R.	D	1-1	Phelan		18,544
24	Feb	3	(h)	Liverpool	D	1-1	Bruce (pen)		43,690
25		26	(a)	Sheffield U	L	1-2	Blackmore (pen)		27,570
26	Mar	2	(h)	Everton	L	0-2			45,656
27		9	(a)	Chelsea	L	2-3	Hughes, McClair		22,818
28		13	(a)	Southampton	D	1-1	Ince		15,701
29		16	(a)	Nottingham F	D	1-1	Blackmore		23,859
30		23	(h)	Luton T	W	4-1	Bruce 2, Robins, McClair		41,752
31		30	(a)	Norwich C	W	3-0	Bruce 2 (1 pen), Ince		18,282
32	Apr	2	(h)	Wimbledon	W	2-1	Bruce, McClair		36,660
33		6	(a)	Aston Villa	D	1-1	Sharpe		33,307
34		16	(h)	Derby Co	W	3-1	Blackmore, McClair, Robson		32,776
35	May	4	(h)	Manchester C	W	1-0	Giggs		45,286
36		6	(a)	Arsenal	L	1-3	Bruce (pen)		40,229
37		11	(a)	Crystal Palace	L	0-3			25,301
38		20	(h)	Tottenham H	D	1-1	Ince		46,791

FINAL LEAGUE POSITION: 6th in Division One

Appearances

Sub. Appearances

Goals

Sealey	Irwin	Donaghy	Bruce	Phelan	Pallister	Webb	Ince	McClair	Hughes	Blackmore	Beardsmore	Robins	Anderson	Sharpe	Martin	Wallace	Robson	Walsh	Ferguson	Giggs	Whitworth	Wratten	Bosnich	Kanchelskis	
1	2	3	4	5	6	7	8	9	10	11															1
1	2	3	4	5	6	7	8*	9	10	11	12														2
1	2	3*	4	5	6	7	8	9	10†	11	12	14													3
1	2	14	4	5	6	7	8	9	12	3	11†	10*													4
1	2		4	5	6	7	8	9		3	11	10													5
1	2	14	4	5	6†	7	8*	9	10	3	12	11													6
1	2†	3		5	6	7		9	10	11	12	8*	4	14											7
1	2		4	5	6	7	8	9	12	3	11†	10*			14										8
1	2†		4	5	6	7	8	9	10	3		12		11*	14										9
1	2		4		6	7	8	9	10	5				11*	3	12									10
1	2		4	5	6	7	8	9		3				11	12	10*									11
1	2†	14	4	5	6	7	8	9	10	3				11*		12									12
1	2*		4	5	6	7	8	9	10	3				11		12									13
1	2		4	5†	6	7	8	9	10	3*				14	12	11									14
1	2		4	5	6	14	8†	9	10	3				7*	12	11									15
1	2*	14	4	5†	6		8	9	10	3				7	11	12									16
1	14		4	5	6	7	8†	9	10	2				3*	11	12									17
1		3	4	5	6	11	8	9	10	2*						12	7								18
1	2	14	4	12	6	5	8	9	10	3				11†			7*								19
1	2		4	12	6	5	8	9	10	3				11			7*								20
1	2†		4	5*	6	7	8	9	10	3	12			11	14										21
1	2		4	12	6	5*	8†	9	10	3				14		11	7								22
1	2	6	4	5			8	9	10	11				7*	12	14	3†								23
1	2		4	5†	6		8*	9	10	3				11	14	12	7								24
	2	5		6	4†		8	9	10		12			3		11	7*	1	14						25
1	2†	5			6		8	9	10		12			7	3*	11			4	14					26
1			4	5	6		8	9	10	2*				11	3	12	7								27
1			4	5	6		8	9	7*		12			11	3	10	14		2†						28
1	2	12	4	5	6		8	10	9	3*				11			7								29
1	2		4	5	6			9	10	3	12			11		8*	7								30
1	2*		4	5	6		8	9	10	3	12	14		11†			7								31
	2	3	4†	5	6	7	8	9	10		12			11*				1		14					32
1	2	3	4	5*	6		8	9	10		12			11			7								33
	2	3	4	6	5*		8	10	9		12			11			7	1							34
	2	12	4	5	6		8	9	10	3							7	1		11*					35
		6	4	2	5		8	9	10*	3	12			11			7†	1	14						36
	2	3	4	6*	5		8	9†	10		12			11			7	1				14			37
	2†	14	4	5	6		8	9	10	3	12			11*			7	1							38
31	33	17	31	30	36	31	31	34	29	35	5	7	1	20	7	13	15	5	2	1	1	2	1		
	1	8		3	1		2	2		7	12			3	7	6	2		3	1		2			
		13	1		3	3	13	10	4		4		2		3	1		1							

1991-92

1	Aug	17	(h)	Notts Co	W	2-0	Hughes, Robson	46,278
2		21	(a)	Aston Villa	W	1-0	Bruce (pen)	39,995
3		24	(a)	Everton	D	0-0		36,085
4		28	(h)	Oldham Ath	W	1-0	McClair	42,078
5		31	(h)	Leeds U	D	1-1	Robson	43,778
6	Sep	3	(a)	Wimbledon	W	2-1	Blackmore, Pallister	13,824
7		7	(h)	Norwich C	W	3-0	Irwin, McClair, Giggs	44,946
8		14	(a)	Southampton	W	1-0	Hughes	19,264
9		21	(h)	Luton T	W	5-0	Ince, Bruce (pen), McClair 2, Hughes	46,491
10		28	(a)	Tottenham H	W	2-1	Hughes, Robson	35,087
11	Oct	6	(h)	Liverpool	D	0-0		44,997
12		19	(h)	Arsenal	D	1-1	Bruce	46,594
13		26	(a)	Sheffield W	L	2-3	McClair 2	38,260
14	Nov	2	(h)	Sheffield U	W	2-0	Beesley (og), Kanchelskis	42,942
15		16	(a)	Manchester C	D	0-0		38,180
16		23	(h)	West Ham U	W	2-1	Giggs, Robson	47,185
17		30	(a)	Crystal Palace	W	3-1	Webb, McClair, Kanchelskis	29,017
18	Dec	7	(h)	Coventry C	W	4-0	Bruce, Webb, McClair, Hughes	42,549
19		15	(a)	Chelsea	W	3-1	Irwin, McClair, Bruce (pen)	23,120
20		26	(a)	Oldham Ath	W	6-3	Irwin 2, Kanchelskis, McClair 2, Giggs	18,947
21		29	(a)	Leeds U	D	1-1	Webb	32,638
22	Jan	1	(h)	Q.P.R.	L	1-4	McClair	38,554
23		11	(h)	Everton	W	1-0	Kanchelskis	46,619
24		18	(a)	Notts Co	D	1-1	Blackmore (pen)	21,055
25		22	(h)	Aston Villa	W	1-0	Hughes	45,022
26	Feb	1	(a)	Arsenal	D	1-1	McClair	41,703
27		8	(h)	Sheffield W	D	1-1	McClair	47,074
28		22	(h)	Crystal Palace	W	2-0	Hughes 2	46,347
29		26	(h)	Chelsea	D	1-1	Hughes	44,872
30		29	(a)	Coventry C	D	0-0		23,967
31	Mar	14	(a)	Sheffield U	W	2-1	McClair, Blackmore	30,183
32		18	(a)	Nottingham F	L	0-1		28,062
33		21	(h)	Wimbledon	D	0-0		45,428
34		28	(a)	Q.P.R.	D	0-0		22,603
35		31	(a)	Norwich C	W	3-1	Ince 2, McClair	17,489
36	Apr	7	(h)	Manchester C	D	1-1	Giggs	46,781
37		16	(h)	Southampton	W	1-0	Kanchelskis	43,972
38		18	(a)	Luton T	D	1-1	Sharpe	13,410
39		20	(h)	Nottingham F	L	1-2	McClair	47,576
40		22	(a)	West Ham U	L	0-1		24,197
41		26	(a)	Liverpool	L	0-2		38,669
42	May	2	(h)	Tottenham H	W	3-1	McClair, Hughes 2	44,595

FINAL LEAGUE POSITION: 2nd in Division One

Appearances

Sub. Appearances

Goals

Schmeichel	Irwin	Blackmore	Bruce	Ferguson	Parker	Robson	Ince	McClair	Hughes	Kanchelskis	Pallister	Giggs	Donaghy	Webb	Phelan	Martin	Robins	Sharpe	Walsh	
1	2	3	4	5†	6	7	8*	9	10	11	12	14								1
1	2	3	4		6	7	8	9	10	11			5							2
1	2†	3*	4		6	7	8	9	10		14	11	5	12						3
1	3	12	4	14	2	7	8*	9	10		6	11		5†						4
1	3	11	4†		2	7	8*	9	10		6	12		5	14					5
1	12	11	4		2	7		9	10		6	3	8	5*						6
1	3	12	4		2	7		9	10	8*	6	11		5†	14					7
1	3		4			7	12	9	10	8*	6	11		5	2					8
1	3	9*	4			7	8	12	10		6	11		5	2					9
1	3	12	4			7	8	9	10	5*	6	11			2					10
1	3	5	4			7	8†	9	10	12	6	11	14	2*						11
1	3	2	4			7	8	9	10	12	6	11		5*						12
1	3	10	4*		2	7		9		8	6	11		5	12					13
	3		4		2	12	8	9	7*	14	11†	6		5			10			14
1	3	8	4		2	7	12	9	10		6	11		5*						15
1	3	12	4		2*	7		9	10	8	6	11		5						16
1	3*	12	4		2	7		9	10	8	6	11		5						17
1	3	12	4		2*		8	9	10	7	6	11		5						18
1	3	12	4		2		8	9	10	7	6	11*		5						19
1	3*	12	4		2	7†	8	9	10	11	6	14		5						20
1		3*	4		2		8	9	10	7†	6	11	14	5				12		21
1		3	4		2		8	9	10		6	12		5	7*			11		22
1		3*	4		2		8	9	10	7	6	11	12	5						23
1	3	12	4*		2		8	9	10	7	6	11†		5			14			24
1	3		4			7	8	9	10	11	6		2	5						25
1	3		4			7	8*	9	10	11	6	12	2	5						26
1	3					7	8	9	10	11	6	2*	5	5†	14			12		27
1	3		14			7	8	9	10	11*	6	4	2	5†				12		28
	3	12	14			7†	8	9	10	11*	6	4	2	5					1	29
	3	12			2		8	9	10	7*	6	11	4	5					1	30
1	3	12	4*		2	7	8	9		11	6			5				10		31
1	3	2	4				8	9	10*	12	6	14		5†	7			11		32
1	3	2	4				8	9	10	7	6	11		5*				12		33
1	3		4			7		9	10	8*	6	11	2	5				12		34
1	3	12	4			7*	8	9	10		6	5	2					11		35
1	3	5*	4				8	9	10	12	6	7	2					11		36
1	3		4		2		8*	9	10	7	6	11	12	5						37
1	3	14	4		2†			9	10*	12	6	7	8	5				11		38
1	3	2	4					9	12	7	6	10	14	8*	5			11†		39
1	2	8*	4	14				9	10	12	6	7	3†	5				11		40
1	2		4			7	8	9	10	5	6*	11	3					12		41
1	3		4		2		8*	9	10	7		11	6	5				12		42
40	37	19	37	2	24	26	31	41	38	28	37	32	16	29	14	1	8	2		
	1	14		2	2	1	2	1	1	6	3	6	4	2	4	1	1	6		
		4	3		5	4	3	18	11	5	1	4		3				1		

1992-93

1	Aug	15	(a)	Sheffield U	L	1-2	Hughes	28,070
2		19	(h)	Everton	L	0-3		31,901
3		22	(h)	Ipswich T	D	1-1	Irwin	31,704
4		24	(a)	Southampton	W	1-0	Dublin	15,623
5		29	(a)	Nottingham F	W	2-0	Hughes, Giggs	19,694
6	Sep	2	(h)	Crystal Palace	W	1-0	Hughes	29,736
7		6	(h)	Leeds U	W	2-0	Kanchelskis, Bruce	31,296
8		12	(a)	Everton	W	2-0	McClair, Bruce (pen)	30,002
9		19	(a)	Tottenham H	D	1-1	Giggs	33,296
10		26	(h)	Q.P.R.	D	0-0		33,287
11	Oct	3	(a)	Middlesbrough	D	1-1	Bruce (pen)	24,172
12		18	(h)	Liverpool	D	2-2	Hughes 2	33,243
13		24	(a)	Blackburn R	D	0-0		20,305
14		31	(h)	Wimbledon	L	0-1		32,622
15	Nov	7	(a)	Aston Villa	L	0-1		39,063
16		21	(h)	Oldham Ath	W	3-0	McClair, Hughes	33,497
17		28	(a)	Arsenal	W	1-0	Hughes	29,739
18	Dec	6	(h)	Manchester C	W	2-1	Ince, Hughes	35,408
19		12	(h)	Norwich C	W	1-0	Hughes	34,500
20		19	(a)	Chelsea	D	1-1	Cantona	34,464
21		26	(a)	Sheffield W	D	3-3	McClair 2, Cantona	37,708
22		28	(h)	Coventry C	W	5-0	Giggs, Hughes, Cantona (pen), Sharpe, Irwin	36,025
23	Jan	9	(h)	Tottenham H	W	4-1	Cantona, Irwin, McClair, Parker	35,648
24		18	(a)	Q.P.R.	W	3-1	Ince, Giggs, Kanchelskis	21,177
25		27	(h)	Nottingham F	W	2-0	Ince, Hughes	36,085
26		30	(a)	Ipswich T	L	1-2	McClair	22,068
27	Feb	6	(h)	Sheffield U	W	2-1	McClair, Cantona	36,156
28		8	(a)	Leeds U	D	0-0		34,166
29		20	(h)	Southampton	W	2-1	Giggs 2	36,257
30		27	(h)	Middlesbrough	W	3-0	Giggs, Irwin, Cantona	36,251
31	Mar	6	(a)	Liverpool	W	2-1	Hughes, McClair	44,374
32		9	(a)	Oldham Ath	L	0-1		17,106
33		14	(h)	Aston Villa	D	1-1	Hughes	36,163
34		20	(a)	Manchester C	D	1-1	Cantona	37,136
35		24	(h)	Arsenal	D	0-0		37,301
36	Apr	5	(a)	Norwich C	W	3-1	Giggs, Kanchelskis, Cantona	20,582
37		10	(h)	Sheffield W	W	2-1	Bruce 2	40,102
38		12	(a)	Coventry C	W	1-0	Irwin	24,429
39		17	(h)	Chelsea	W	3-0	Hughes, Clarke (og), Cantona	40,139
40		21	(a)	Crystal Palace	W	2-0	Hughes, Ince	30,115
41	May	3	(h)	Blackburn R	W	3-1	Giggs, Ince, Pallister	40,447
42		9	(a)	Wimbledon	W	2-1	Ince, Robson	30,115

FINAL LEAGUE POSITION: 1st in Premier League

Appearances

Sub. Appearances

Goals

Schmeichel	Irwin	Blackmore	Bruce	Ferguson	Pallister	Kanchelskis	Ince	McClair	Hughes	Giggs	Phelan	Dublin	Webb	Wallace	Robson	Parker	Sharpe	Butt	Cantona	Match
1	2	3	4	5	6	7†	8*	9	10	11	12	14								1
1	2	3	4	5	6	7	8*	9	10	11†	12	14								2
1	2	3†	4	5	6	7*		9	10	11	8	12	14							3
1	3		4	5	6		8	9	10	11	2	7								4
1	3	14	4	5	6	12	8	9	10*	11	2†	7								5
1	3	2	4	5	6	12	8	9	10	11		7*								6
1	3	2	4	5	6	7	8	9	10	11										7
1	2	3	4	5	6	7	8	9	10	11										8
1	2	3	4	5	6	7*	8	9	10	11		12					'			9
1	2	3	4	5	6	7*	8	9	10	11		12								10
1	2	7	4	5	6	12	8	9	10†	11	3*			14						11
1	3	12	4	5	6	7*	8	9	10	11†						2				12
1	3	7	4	5*	6	12	8	9	10	11						2				13
1	3		4	5	6	7*	8	9	10	11			12			2				14
1	3		4	5*	6		8	12	10	11					7	2	9			15
1	3*		4		6		8†	9	10	11	12				7	2	5	14		16
1	3		4		6		8	9	10	11					7	2	5			17
1	3		4		6		8	9	10	11*					7	2	5		12	18
1	3		4		6		8	9	10	11						2	5		7	19
1	3		4		6	12	8	9	10		5*					2	11		7	20
1	3		4		6	12	8	9	10	11*						2	5		7	21
1	3		4†		6	12	8	9	10	11*	14					2	5		7	22
1	3		4		6	12	8†	9	10	11*	14					2	5		7	23
1	3		4		6	7	8	9	10*	11	12					2	5			24
1	3		4		6		8	9	10	11						2	5		7	25
1	3		4		6	12	8	9	10	11						2	5*		7	26
1	3		4		6		8	9	10	11*						2	5		7	27
1	3		4		6		8	9	10	11*						2	5		7	28
1	3		4		6		8	9	10	11						2	5		7	29
1	3		4		6		8	9	10	11						2	5		7	30
1	3		4		6	7	8	9	10	11						2	5			31
1	3		4		6	7*	8	9	10	11	12					2	5			32
1	3		4		6		8	9	10	11						2	5		7	33
1	3		4		6		8	9	10	11						2	5		7	34
1	3		4		6		8	9	10*	11					12	2	5		7	35
1	3		4	10*	6		8	9		11					12	2	5		7	36
1	3		4		6		8	9	10	11					12	2*	5		7	37
1	3		4		6		8	9	10	11					12	2	5		7*	38
1	3		4	14	6		8	9*	10	11†					12	2	5		7	39
1	3		4	5*	6		8	9	10	11					12	2			7	40
1	3		4	14	6		8	9†	10	11					12	2	5*		7	41
1	3*		4		6		8	9	10	12					7	2	5		11	42
42	40	12	42	15	42	14	41	41	41	40	5	3			5	31	27		21	
		2				13		1		1	6	4	1	2	9			1	1	
	5		5		1	3	6	9	15	9	1				1	1	1		9	

1993-94

1	Aug	15	(a)	Norwich C	W	2-0	Robson, Giggs		19,705
2		18	(h)	Sheffield U	W	3-0	Keane 2, Hughes		41,949
3		21	(h)	Newcastle U	D	1-1	Giggs		41,829
4		23	(a)	Aston Villa	W	2-1	Sharpe 2		39,624
5		28	(a)	Southampton	W	3-1	Irwin, Sharpe, Cantona		16,189
6	Sep	1	(h)	West Ham U	W	3-0	Bruce, Sharpe, Cantona		44,613
7		11	(a)	Chelsea	L	0-1			37,064
8		19	(h)	Arsenal	W	1-0	Cantona		44,009
9		25	(h)	Swindon T	W	4-2	Cantona, Hughes 2, Kanchelskis		44,583
10	Oct	2	(a)	Sheffield W	W	3-2	Hughes 2, Giggs		34,548
11		16	(h)	Tottenham H	W	2-1	Sharpe, Keane		44,655
12		23	(a)	Everton	W	1-0	Sharpe		35,430
13		30	(h)	Q.P.R.	W	2-1	Cantona, Hughes		44,663
14	Nov	7	(a)	Manchester C	W	3-2	Cantona 2, Keane		35,155
15		20	(h)	Wimbledon	W	3-1	Pallister, Hughes, Kanchelskis		44,748
16		24	(h)	Ipswich T	D	0-0			43,300
17		27	(a)	Coventry C	W	1-0	Cantona		17,020
18	Dec	4	(h)	Norwich C	D	2-2	McClair, Giggs		44,694
19		7	(a)	Sheffield U	W	3-0	Sharpe, Cantona, Hughes		26,746
20		11	(a)	Newcastle U	D	1-1	Ince		36,388
21		19	(h)	Aston Villa	W	3-1	Cantona 2, Ince		44,499
22		26	(h)	Blackburn R	D	1-1	Ince		44,511
23		29	(a)	Oldham Ath	W	5-2	Bruce, Cantona, Kanchelskis, Giggs 2		16,708
24	Jan	1	(h)	Leeds U	D	0-0			44,724
25		4	(a)	Liverpool	D	3-3	Irwin, Bruce, Giggs		42,795
26		15	(a)	Tottenham H	W	1-0	Hughes		31,343
27		22	(h)	Everton	W	1-0	Giggs		44,750
28	Feb	5	(a)	Q.P.R.	W	3-2	Kanchelskis, Cantona, Giggs		21,267
29		26	(a)	West Ham U	D	2-2	Ince, Hughes		28,832
30	Mar	5	(h)	Chelsea	L	0-1			44,745
31		14	(h)	Sheffield W	W	5-0	Cantona 2, Ince, Hughes, Giggs		43,669
32		19	(a)	Swindon T	D	2-2	Keane, Ince		18,102
33		22	(a)	Arsenal	D	2-2	Sharpe 2		36,203
34		30	(h)	Liverpool	W	1-0	Ince		44,751
35	Apr	2	(a)	Blackburn R	L	0-2			20,886
36		4	(h)	Oldham Ath	W	3-2	Ince, Giggs, Dublin		44,686
37		16	(a)	Wimbledon	L	0-1			28,553
38		23	(h)	Manchester C	W	2-0	Cantona 2		44,333
39		27	(a)	Leeds U	W	2-0	Kanchelskis, Giggs		41,125
40	May	1	(a)	Ipswich T	W	2-1	Cantona, Giggs		22,559
41		4	(h)	Southampton	W	2-0	Kanchelskis, Hughes		44,705
42		8	(h)	Coventry City	D	0-0			44,717

FINAL LEAGUE POSITION: 1st in F.A. Premiership

Appearances

Sub. Appearances

Goals

Schmeichel	Parker	Irwin	Bruce	Kanchelskis	Pallister	Robson	Ince	Keane	Hughes	Giggs	McClair	Sharpe	Cantona	Butt	Martin	Phelan	Ferguson	Thornley	Dublin	Walsh	Neville G	McKee	No.
1	2	3	4	5	6	7	8	9	10	11													
1	2	3	4	5	6	7	8	9	10	11	12												1
1	2	3	4	5	6	7	8	9	10	11	14	12											2
1	2	3	4	7	6		8	9	10	11		5											3
1	2	3	4	14	6		8	9	10	11	12	5	7										4
1	2	3	4	10	6	14	8	9		11	12	5	7										5
1	2	3	4		6	10	8	9		11	12	5	7										6
1	2	3	4		6		8	9	10	11	12	5	7										7
1	2	3	4	11	6		8	9	10	14	12	5	7										8
1	2	3	4	12	6		8	9	10	11		5	7										9
1	2	3	4		6		8	9	10	11	12	5	7	14									10
1		3	4		6		8	11	10		9	5	7		2								11
1	2	3	4				8	9	10	11		5	7			6							12
1	2	3	4	11	6		8	9	10	14		5	7										13
1	2	3	4	11	6	9	8		10			5	7				12						14
1	2	3	4	11	6	9	8		10			5	7					12					15
1	2	3	4		6		8		10	11		5	7					12					16
1	2	3	4		6		8		10	11		5	7					9					17
1	2	3	4	5	6		8		10	11	9	14	7										18
1	2	3	4		6		8	12	10	11	9	5	7										19
1	2	3	4	12	6		8	14	10	11	9	5	7										20
1	2	3	4	11	6		8	9	10		12	5	7										21
1	2	3	4		6		8	9	10	11	12	5	7				14						22
1	2	3	4	10	6	14	8	9		11	12	5	7										23
1	2	3	4	10	6	5		8		11	9	7											24
1	2	3	4	10	6		8	5		11	9	7											25
1	2	3	4	5	6		8	9	10	11	12	7											26
1	2	3	4	5	6		8	9	10	11		7											27
1	2	3	4	5	6		8	9	10	11		7											28
1	2	3	4	5	6		8	11	10		9	7						12	14				29
1	2	3	4	5	6	12	8	7	10	11	9								14				30
1	2	3	4	5	6	14	8	9	10	11	12	7											31
1	2	3	4		6		8	5	10	11	9	7											32
1	2	3	4		6		8	9	10	11	12	5	7										33
1	2	3	4	11	6	14	8	9	10		12	5	7										34
1	2	3	4	7	6		8	9	10	11	12	5											35
1		3	4	7	6		8	2	10	11	9	5						12					36
1	2	3	4	5	6	7	8		10	11	9	12						14					37
1	2	3	4	11	6		8	9	10		12	5	7										38
1	2	3	4	5	6		8	9	10	11		7											39
1	2	3	4	5	6		8	9	10	11		14	7						12				40
	2	3		4	6		8	9	10	11		5	7						1				41
	12	3	4		6	10		14			9	5	7					11	1	2	8		42
40	39	42	41	28	41	10	39	34	36	32	12	26	34	-	1	1	1	-	1	2	1	1	
	1		3		5		3			6	14	4		1		1	2	1	4	1			
		2	3	6	1	1	8	5	12	13	1	9	18					1					

1994-95

1 Aug	20	(h)	Q.P.R.	W	2-0	Hughes, McClair	43,214
2	22	(a)	Nottingham F	D	1-1	Kanchelskis	22,072
3	27	(a)	Tottenham H	W	1-0	Bruce	24,502
4	31	(h)	Wimbledon	W	3-0	Cantona, McClair, Giggs	43,440
5 Sep	11	(a)	Leeds U	L	1-2	Cantona (pen)	39,120
6	17	(h)	Liverpool	W	2-0	Kanchelskis, McClair	43,740
7	24	(a)	Ipswich T	L	2-3	Cantona, Scholes	22,553
8 Oct	1	(h)	Everton	W	2-0	Kanchelskis, Sharpe	43,803
9	8	(a)	Sheffield W	L	0-1		32,616
10	15	(h)	West Ham U	W	1-0	Cantona	4,379
11	23	(a)	Blackburn R	W	4-2	Cantona (pen), Kanchelskis 2, Hughes	30,260
12	29	(h)	Newcastle U	W	2-0	Pallister, Gillespie	43,795
13 Nov	6	(a)	Aston Villa	W	2-1	Ince, Kanchelskis	32,136
14	10	(h)	Manchester C	W	5-0	Cantona, Kanchelskis 3, Hughes	43,738
15	19	(h)	Crystal Palace	W	3-0	Irwin, Cantona, Kanchelskis	43,788
16	26	(a)	Arsenal	D	0-0		38,301
17 Dec	3	(h)	Norwich C	W	1-0	Cantona	43,789
18	10	(a)	Q.P.R.	W	3-2	Scholes 2, Keane	18,948
19	17	(h)	Nottingham F	L	1-2	Cantona	43,744
20	26	(a)	Chelsea	W	3-2	Hughes, Cantona (pen), McClair	31,139
21	28	(h)	Leicester C	D	1-1	Kanchelskis	43,789
22	31	(a)	Southampton	D	2-2	Butt, Pallister	15,204
23 Jan	3	(h)	Coventry C	W	2-0	Scholes, Cantona (pen)	43,120
24	15	(a)	Newcastle U	D	1-1	Hughes	34,471
25	22	(h)	Blackburn R	W	1-0	Cantona	43,742
26	25	(a)	Crystal Palace	D	1-1	May	18,224
27 Feb	4	(h)	Aston Villa	W	1-0	Cole	43,795
28	11	(a)	Manchester C	W	3-0	Ince, Kanchelskis, Cole	26,368
29	22	(a)	Norwich C	W	2-0	Ince, Kanchelskis	21,824
30	25	(a)	Everton	L	0-1		40,011
31 Mar	4	(h)	Ipswich T	W	9-0	Keane, Cole 5, Hughes 2, Ince	43,804
32	7	(a)	Wimbledon	W	1-0	Bruce	18,224
33	15	(h)	Tottenham H	D	0-0		43,802
34	19	(h)	Liverpool	L	0-2		38,906
35	22	(h)	Arsenal	W	3-0	Hughes, Sharpe, Kanchelskis	43,623
36 Apr	2	(h)	Leeds U	D	0-0		43,712
37	15	(a)	Leicester C	W	4-0	Sharpe, Cole 2, Ince	21,281
38	17	(h)	Chelsea	D	0-0		43,728
39 May	1	(a)	Coventry C	W	3-2	Scholes, Cole 2	21,858
40	7	(h)	Sheffield W	W	1-0	May	43,868
41	10	(h)	Southampton	W	2-1	Cole, Irwin (pen)	43,479
42	14	(a)	West Ham U	D	1-1	McClair	24,783

FINAL LEAGUE POSITION: 2nd in F.A. Carling Premiership

Appearances

Sub. Appearances

Goals

Schmeichel	May	Irwin	Bruce	Sharpe	Pallister	Kanchelskis	Ince	McClair	Hughes	Giggs	Parker	Keane	Cantona	Walsh	Scholes	Butt	Gillespie	Davies	Pilkington	Neville G	Cole	Neville P	Beckham	No.
1	2*	3	4	5†	6	7	8		10	11		12	14											1
1	2	3	4	5	6	7	8	9	10	11*		12												2
1	2	3	4	5	6	7	8	9	10	11														3
1	2	3	4	5	6		8	9	10	11			7											4
1	2	3	4	12	6	5	8	9†	10	11*		7	14											5
1	2	3	4	5	6	7	8	12	10*	11			9											6
	2	4	3*		6	7	8	9†		11		5	10	1	12	14								7
1	2	3	4	5	6	11	8	12	10*			9	7											8
1	12	3	4	5	6		8	9	10		2*		7		14		11†							9
1	2*	3	4	5	6	7	8		10	11			9		12									10
1		3	4	5	6	7	8	12	10			2	9		11*									11
1		3	4		6	5	8	9	10	11*		2	7		12									12
		3	4		6	5	8	12		11		2	9	1	7†	10*	14							13
1		3	4		6	5	8	9	10	11*		2	7		12									14
1°	4	3		6	5*		8	9	10			7	14		12		11†	15		2				15
	4	3		6	5*		8	9	10				7	1	12		11†	14		2				16
	4	3		6	5†		8	9	10				7	1	14	12	11*			2				17
		3	4		6	7	8	9				5		1	10	14	12	11†		2*				18
		3	4	5†	6		8	9	10	11*		2	7	1	12					14				19
		3	4	12	6		8†	9	10	11		2	7	1	5*					14				20
		3	4	5	6			9	10*	11		8	7	1	12					2				21
	2	4			6			9*	10	11		5	7	1	8	12				3				22
		3	4	12						11		8*	7	1	9	10	5			2				23
1	12	3	4	5	6			9	10†	11		2	7		14	8*								24
1		3	4	5*	6	12	8	9		11		2	7								10			25
1	4	3		5*	6	12	8	9		11		2	7								10			26
1	12	3	4	5	6	14	8	9		11†										2*	10			27
1	12	3	4	5	6	7*	8	9		11					14						10	2†		28
1	4	3		5	6		8	9	10	11										2	7			29
1	2	4	3		6	12	8	9*	10	11		5									7			30
1		3	4†	12	6	5	8	9	10	11		2*			14						7			31
1		3	4	5	6		8	9	10	11										2	7			32
1	2	4	3	5	6		8	9*	10	11						12					7			33
1	2	4	3*		6	7	8	9	10	11		5†			14					12				34
1		3	4	5	6	7	8		10	11										2	9			35
1		3			6		8	9	10	11		5								2	7		4	36
1		3	4	5†	6		8	10*							12	11				2	7		14	37
1		3	4		6		8	9							12	11		14*		2	7		5†	38
1	4	3		5	6			9	10						11*	7				2	8		12	39
1	4†	3		5	6		8	9	10						11*	12				2	7	14		40
1		3	4	5	6		8	9	10*						12	11				2	7			41
1		3	4	5	6		8	9	12			10†			14	11*				2	7			42
32	15	40	35	26	42	25	36	35	33	29	1	23	21	10	6	11	3	3		16	17	1	2	
	4		2	5			5	1			1	2			11	11	6	2	1	2	1	1	2	
	2	2	2	3	2	14	5	5	8	1		2	12		5	1		1			12			

59

1995-96

1 Aug	19	(a)	Aston Villa	L	1-3	Beckham	34,655
2	23	(h)	West Ham U	W	2-1	Scholes, Keane	31,966
3	26	(h)	Wimbledon	W	3-1	Keane 2, Cole	32,226
4	28	(a)	Blackburn R	W	2-1	Sharpe, Beckham	29,843
5 Sep	9	(a)	Everton	W	3-2	Sharpe 2, Giggs	39,496
6	16	(h)	Bolton W	W	3-0	Scholes 2, Giggs	32,812
7	23	(a)	Sheffield W	D	0-0		34,101
8 Oct	1	(h)	Liverpool	D	2-2	Butt, Cantona (pen)	34,934
9	14	(h)	Manchester C	W	1-0	Scholes	35,707
10	21	(a)	Chelsea	W	4-1	Scholes 2, Giggs, McClair	30,192
11	28	(h)	Middlesbrough	W	2-0	Pallister, Cole	36,580
12 Nov	4	(a)	Arsenal	L	0-1		38,317
13	18	(h)	Southampton	W	4-1	Giggs 2, Scholes, Cole	39,301
14	22	(a)	Coventry C	W	4-0	Irwin, McClair 2, Beckham	23,344
15	27	(a)	Nottingham F	D	1-1	Cantona (pen)	29,263
16 Dec	2	(h)	Chelsea	D	1-1	Beckham	42,019
17	9	(h)	Sheffield W	D	2-2	Cantona 2	41,849
18	17	(a)	Liverpool	L	0-2		40,546
19	24	(a)	Leeds U	L	1-3	Cole	39,801
20	27	(h)	Newcastle U	W	2-0	Cole, Keane	42,024
21	30	(h)	Q.P.R.	W	2-1	Cole, Giggs	41,890
22 Jan	1	(a)	Tottenham H	L	1-4	Cole	32,852
23	13	(h)	Aston Villa	D	0-0		42,667
24	22	(a)	West Ham U	W	1-0	Cantona	24,197
25 Feb	3	(a)	Wimbledon	W	4-2	Cole, Perry (og), Cantona 2 (1 pen)	25,423
26	10	(h)	Blackburn R	W	1-0	Sharpe	42,681
27	21	(h)	Everton	W	2-0	Keane, Giggs	42,459
28	25	(a)	Bolton W	W	6-0	Beckham, Bruce, Cole, Scholes 2, Butt	21,381
29 Mar	4	(a)	Newcastle U	W	1-0	Cantona	36,584
30	16	(a)	Q.P.R.	D	1-1	Cantona	18,817
31	20	(h)	Arsenal	W	1-0	Cantona	50,028
32	24	(h)	Tottenham H	W	1-0	Cantona	50,508
33 Apr	6	(a)	Manchester C	W	3-2	Cantona (pen), Cole, Giggs	29,688
34	8	(h)	Coventry C	W	1-0	Cantona	50,332
35	13	(a)	Southampton	L	1-3	Giggs	15,262
36	17	(h)	Leeds U	W	1-0	Keane	48,382
37	28	(h)	Nottingham F	W	5-0	Scholes, Beckham 2, Giggs, Cantona	53,926
38 May	5	(a)	Middlesbrough	W	3-0	May, Cole, Giggs	29,922

FINAL LEAGUE POSITION: 1st in F.A. Carling Premiership

Appearances

Sub. Appearances

Goals

Schmeichel	Neville P	Irwin	Parker	Neville G	Pallister	Butt	Keane	McClair	Scholes	Sharpe	Beckham	O'Kane	Bruce	Cole	Thornley	Giggs	Davies	Cooke	Cantona	May	Pilkington	Prunier	
1	2*	3	4	5	6†	7	8	9	10	11	12	13											1
1		3		2	6	7	8	9†	10*	5	11		4	12	13								2
1		3		2	6	7	8		10†	5	11		4	9*		12	13						3
1		3		2	6	7	8		10*	5	11†		4	9		12	13						4
1		3		2	6	7	8		10*	5	11		4	9†		12	13						5
1		3		2	6	7		9	5	10			4			11	12		8*				6
1		3		2	6	7	5	9		10			4			11		8*	12				7
1		3*		2	6	10†	8	12	5	13			4	9		11			7				8
1		3		2	6	7	5*	12	10†	13	8		4	9		11							9
1		3		2	6	8	5	12	10*				4	9		11			7				10
1		3		2	6	8	5	12	10*				4	9		11			7				11
1		3†		2	6	8*	5	13	10°	12	14		4	9		11			7				12
1	12	3*		2	6	8		13	10†	14	5		4	9		11°			7				13
1	12	3		2*	6	10†	8	13	5				4°	9		11			7	14			14
1		3		2	6	5	8*	12	13	10†			4	9		11			7				15
		3		2		8		10	5	11			4	9*		12			7	6	1		16
	3			2		8		10*	5†	11			4	9		12	13		7	6	1		17
1		3		2		8		12	5	10			4	9*		11			7	6			18
1	13	3	6°	2			10	5	8	12	11*		4†	9					7	14			19
1	2	3			6		10	8	12	5				9		11			7	4*			20
1		3*	12	2	6		10	5	13		14		8°	9†		11			7	4			21
1°		3†	4	2			10	5*	12	13	8			9		11			7		14	6	22
1		3		2	6		10	8	12	5*			4	9		11			7				23
1	6	3		2			10	8	5	12			4	9*		11			7				24
1		3		2	6		10	8	5	12			4*	9		11			7				25
1		3		2	6		8		5	10				9		11			7	4			26
1		3		2	6		10	8	5*	12			4	9		11			7				27
1		3		2	6		10	8	12	13	5		4	9		11*			7†				28
1		3		2	6		10	8	5				4	9		11			7				29
1		3		2	12	5	8†	13	14	10°			4	9		11			7	6*			30
1		3		2			10	8	12	5			4	9*		11			7	6			31
1		3†		2			10	8	12	5	13		4	9*		11			7	6			32
1		3		2	6		10	5	12	8			4†	9*		11			7	13			33
1				2	5		10	8		3			4	9		11			7	6			34
1				2	5		10*	8	12	3†	6		4	9		11			7	13			35
1		3		2	6		5	8*	12	13	10		4°	9†		11			7	14			36
1		3*	12	2	6		8	9	5	10						11			7	4			37
1		3		2	6		10	5	9*	8				12		11			7	4			38
35	21	31	5	30	21	31	29	12	16	21	26		30	32		30	1	1	30	11	2	2	
	3		1	1		1		10	10	10	7	1		2	1	3	5	3		5	1		
		1			1	2	6	3	10	4	7		1	11		11			14	1			

1996-97

1 Aug	17	(a)	Wimbledon	W	3-0	Cantona, Irwin, Beckham	25,786
2	21	(h)	Everton	D	2-2	Cruyff, Unsworth (og)	54,943
3	25	(h)	Blackburn R	D	2-2	Cruyff, Solskjaer	54,178
4 Sep	4	(a)	Derby Co	D	1-1	Beckham	18,025
5	7	(a)	Leeds U	W	4-0	Martyn (og), Butt, Poborsky, Cantona	39,694
6	14	(h)	Nottingham F	W	4-1	Solskjaer, Giggs, Cantona 2 (1 pen)	54,984
7	21	(a)	Aston Villa	D	0-0		39,339
8	29	(h)	Tottenham H	W	2-0	Solskjaer 2	54,943
9 Oct	12	(h)	Liverpool	W	1-0	Beckham	55,128
10	20	(a)	Newcastle U	L	0-5		36,579
11	26	(a)	Southampton	L	3-6	Beckham, May, Scholes	15,256
12 Nov	2	(h)	Chelsea	L	1-2	May	55,198
13	16	(h)	Arsenal	W	1-0	Winterburn (og)	55,210
14	23	(a)	Middlesbrough	D	2-2	Keane, May	30,063
15	30	(h)	Leicester C	W	3-1	Butt 2, Solskjaer	55,196
16 Dec	8	(a)	West Ham U	D	2-2	Solskjaer, Beckham	25,045
17	18	(a)	Sheffield W	D	1-1	Scholes	37,671
18	21	(h)	Sunderland	W	5-0	Solskjaer 2, Cantona 2 (1 pen), Butt	55,081
19	26	(a)	Nottingham F	W	4-0	Beckham, Butt, Solskjaer, Cole	29,032
20	28	(h)	Leeds U	W	1-0	Cantona (pen)	55,256
21 Jan	1	(h)	Aston Villa	D	0-0		55,133
22	12	(a)	Tottenham H	W	2-1	Solskjaer, Beckham	33,026
23	18	(a)	Coventry C	W	2-0	Giggs, Solskjaer	23,080
24	29	(h)	Wimbledon	W	2-1	Giggs, Cole	55,314
25 Feb	1	(h)	Southampton	W	2-1	Pallister, Cantona	55,269
26	19	(a)	Arsenal	W	2-1	Cole, Solskjaer	38,172
27	22	(a)	Chelsea	D	1-1	Beckham	28,324
28 Mar	1	(h)	Coventry C	W	3-1	Breen (og), Cole, Poborsky	55,230
29	8	(a)	Sunderland	L	1-2	Melville (og)	22,204
30	15	(h)	Sheffield W	W	2-0	Cole, Poborsky	55,267
31	22	(a)	Everton	W	2-0	Solskjaer, Cantona	40,079
32 Apr	5	(h)	Derby Co	L	2-3	Cantona, Solskjaer	55,243
33	12	(a)	Blackburn R	W	3-2	Cole, Scholes, Cantona	30,476
34	19	(a)	Liverpool	W	3-1	Pallister 2, Cole	40,892
35 May	3	(a)	Leicester C	D	2-2	Solskjaer 2	21,068
36	5	(h)	Middlesbrough	D	3-3	Keane, G. Neville, Solskjaer	54,489
37	8	(h)	Newcastle U	D	0-0		55,236
38	11	(h)	West Ham U	W	2-0	Solskjaer, Cruyff	55,249

FINAL LEAGUE POSITION: 1st in F.A. Carling Premiership

Appearances

Sub. Appearances

Goals

Schmeichel	Irwin	Neville P	May	Keane	Pallister	Cantona	Butt	Scholes	Beckham	Cruyff	Johnsen	McClair	Poborsky	Giggs	Neville G	Solskjaer	Cole	Van der Gouw	Clegg	O'Kane	Thornley	Casper	
1	2	3	4	5	6	7†	8*	9	10	11	12	13											1
1	2	3	4		6	7	8		10	9	12			5*		11							2
1	2	3*	4†		6	7			10	9	5	8		11	12	13							3
1	3		4†		6	7	8	12	10	9*	5			11	2	13							4
1	3	4				7	8	10*	9°	6	12	5†		11	2	13	14						5
1	3				6	7	8*		10	4	12	5		11	2	9†	13						6
	3		5		6	7		10		9*	4	12		11	2	8†	13	1					7
1	3		4		6	7	8	12	10	13	5*			11†	2	9							8
1	3		4			7	8	12	10	11	6	5*		13	2	9†							9
1	3		4		6	7	8	12	10	13	5*		14	11°	2	9†							10
1	12	3	4	5	6*	7	8°	9	10	11†			14		2	13							11
1	2	3	4	5		7	8	9*	10		6	12		11									12
1	3		4			7	8		10	6	5			11	2	9							13
1			4	5		7	8	9	10	12	6	13							2	3†	11*		14
1	3	4	5		6	7	8		10	9*	13			11†	2	12							15
1	3	12	4		6	7	8*		10		2	5		11		9							16
1	3	12	4		6	7	8	9		13	5*			11	2†	10							17
1	5	3	4		6†	7	8		10	13	12			11°	2	9*	14						18
1	3		4			7	8†	5	10	6	13	12		11*	2	9°	14						19
1	3		4	5		7	12	8*	10	6				11	2	9†	13						20
1	3		4	5		7	8*	12	10	6				11	2	9†	13						21
1		4	5		6		8*		10		3°		12	11	2	9†	13					14	22
1	3		5		6	7	8	4*	10					11	2	9					12		23
1	3		5		6	7	8*		10	11	4					9	12		2				24
1	3		5		6	7			10	12	8†			11	4	9	13		2*				25
1	3		5		6		12†		10	4	13	8*		11	2	7	9						26
1	3	12	5		6				10	13	4*	8		11†	2	7	9						27
1	3*	12	4		6	7		10°	8	13	14	5		11†	2	9							28
1	3	5	4			7			10	11†	6	9		8*	2	12	13						29
1	3		4		6	7	5	12	10	13				11	2	8*	9†						30
1	2	3	4	5	6*	7	8		10†	12	13			11		9							31
1	12	3	5		6†	7	8°	13	10	4				11	2*	14	9						32
	3		5		6	7	8	10*	12	4	2			11		9		1					33
1	3		5		6	7	8	11*	10		4	12			2	9							34
1	3	4	5		6	7	8*	11		12	13				2	10†	9						35
1	3	4	8		6	7	12		10		5*	2		11		9							36
1	3	4	5†			7	11		10	6	13	8			2	12	9*						37
1	2°	3	4			7	8	11*	10	12	6	13		5†		9	14						38
36	29	15	28	21	27	36	24	16	33	11	26	4	15	25	30	25	10	2	3	1	1		
	2	3	1				2	8	3	5	5	15	7	1	1	8	10		1		1	2	
	1		3	2	3	11	5	3	8	3			3	3	1	18	7						

1997-98

1 Aug	10	(a)	Tottenham H	W 2-0	Butt, Vega (og)	26,359
2	13	(h)	Southampton	W 1-0	Beckham	55,008
3	23	(a)	Leicester C	D 0-0		21,221
4	27	(a)	Everton	W 2-0	Beckham, Sheringham	40,479
5	30	(h)	Coventry C	W 3-0	Cole, Keane, Poborsky	55,074
6 Sep	13	(h)	West Ham U	W 2-1	Keane, Scholes	55,068
7	20	(a)	Bolton W	D 0-0		25,000
8	24	(h)	Chelsea	D 2-2	Scholes, Solskjaer	55,163
9	27	(a)	Leeds U	L 0-1		39,943
10 Oct	4	(h)	Crystal Palace	W 2-0	Sheringham, Hreidarsson (og)	55,143
11	18	(a)	Derby Co	D 2-2	Sheringham, Cole	30,014
12	25	(h)	Barnsley	W 7-0	Cole 3, Giggs 2, Scholes, Poborsky	55,142
13 Nov	1	(h)	Sheffield W	W 6-1	Sheringham 2, Cole 2, Solskjaer 2	55,295
14	9	(a)	Arsenal	L 2-3	Sheringham 2	38,205
15	22	(a)	Wimbledon	W 5-2	Butt, Beckham 2, Scholes, Cole	26,309
16	30	(h)	Blackburn R	W 4-0	Solskjaer 2, Henchoz (og), Kenna (og)	55,175
17 Dec	6	(a)	Liverpool	W 3-1	Cole 2, Beckham	41,027
18	15	(h)	Aston Villa	W 1-0	Giggs	55,175
19	21	(a)	Newcastle U	W 1-0	Cole	36,763
20	26	(h)	Everton	W 2-0	Berg, Cole	55,167
21	28	(a)	Coventry C	L 2-3	Solskjaer, Sheringham	23,055
22 Jan	10	(h)	Tottenham H	W 2-0	Giggs 2	55,281
23	19	(a)	Southampton	L 0-1		15,241
24	31	(h)	Leicester C	L 0-1		55,156
25 Feb	7	(h)	Bolton W	D 1-1	Cole	55,156
26	18	(a)	Aston Villa	W 2-0	Beckham, Giggs	39,372
27	21	(h)	Derby Co	W 2-0	Giggs, Irwin (pen)	55,170
28	28	(a)	Chelsea	W 1-0	Neville P	34,517
29 Mar	7	(a)	Sheffield W	L 0-2		39,427
30	11	(a)	West Ham U	D 1-1	Scholes	25,892
31	14	(h)	Arsenal	L 0-1		55,174
32	28	(h)	Wimbledon	W 2-0	Johnsen, Scholes	55,306
33 Apr	6	(a)	Blackburn R	W 3-1	Cole, Scholes, Beckham	30,547
34	10	(h)	Liverpool	D 1-1	Johnsen	55,171
35	18	(h)	Newcastle U	D 1-1	Beckham	55,194
36	27	(a)	Crystal Palace	W 3-0	Scholes, Butt, Cole	26,180
37 May	4	(h)	Leeds U	W 3-0	Giggs, Irwin (pen), Beckham	55,167
38	10	(a)	Barnsley	W 2-0	Cole, Sheringham	18,694

FINAL LEAGUE POSITION: 2nd in F.A. Carling Premiership

Appearances

Sub. Appearances

Goals

Schmeichel	Irwin	Neville P	Johnsen	Keane	Pallister	Scholes	Butt	Cruyff	Sheringham	Giggs	Beckham	Berg	Neville G	Cole	Poborsky	McClair	Solskjaer	Thornley	Curtis	Wallwork	Pilkington	Nevland	Clegg	Van der Gouw	May	Brown	Mulryne	Higginbotham	
1	2	3	4	5	6	7*	8	9	10	11	12																		1
1	2	3	4†	5	6	7*	8	9	10	11	12	13																	2
1	3			5	6	12	8	9*	10	11	7	4	2																3
1	3			5	6	9	8		10*	11	7	4	2	12															4
1	12	3*		5	6		8		10	11	7	4	2	9†	13														5
1	3			5	6	10	8			11*	7	4	2	9†	12	13													6
1	3	12		5	6	10†	8				7	4	2	9	11*		13												7
1	3			5	6	10°	8		12	13	7	4	2†	9	11*		14												8
1	3	12	13	5	6	8†			10		7	4	2*		11°		9	14											9
1	12	3*	5†		6	9	8		10	11	7	4	2			13													10
1	3*	12	13	6	5°	8†			10	11	7	4	2	14			9												11
1	3			6°	5*	8	12		11	7†		4		9		13	10		2	14									12
1	3			6	5*	8†			10		7	4°	2	9	12	13	11		14										13
1	3	12		6*	5	8			10	11†	7	4	2	9		13													14
1	3	5		6		7	8		10	11	12	4	2*	9															15
1	3	12		6†		8*			10°	11	7	4	2	9	13	14	5												16
1	3	5		6		8			10	11	7	4	2	9															17
1	3	4		6		5			10	11	7		2	9		12	8*												18
1	3	4		6	5†	8			10*	11	7		2	9		12	13												19
	3°		5		6†	11	8				7*	4	2	9	12	13	10		14		1								20
		3†		6	5	12			10	11	7	4	2	9			8*	13			1								21
1	3	4		6		5			10	11	7		2	9			8												22
1	3	4		6		5	8*			11	7		2†	9		12	10					13							23
1	3	12	4†	6	5*	8			14	11	7	13°	2	9			10												24
1	3	2		6	5				10*	11	7	12	4	9			8												25
1	3	12		6		8			10	11	7	4	2	9		5*													26
1	3°	5		6		8	12		10	11†	7	4	2	9*		13									14				27
1	3	5	4	6*	11	8			10		7	12	2	9															28
		5°	6*		12	8	10				7	3	2	9†		13	11		14					1	4				29
1	3				11	8°	10				7	6	2	9*	5†	12	13	14							4				30
1	3	8*	5†		11		10				7	6	4	9		12	14	2°								13			31
	3	8	5		11						7	6	2	9*		12	10†	13						1	4				32
1	3	5	4	6		8	12			11	7		2	9			10*												33
1	3	5*	4†	6		10	8		12	11°	7		2	9				14							13				34
1°	3	5		6	12	8*			10	11	7		2†	9			13							15	4				35
1	3*	2		6	5	8			10	11	7			9										12	4				36
	3*	12		6	5	8			10†	11	7		2	9			13							1	4°	14			37
						8			10	11			2	9				3					6*	1	4	5	7	12	38
32	23	24	18	9	33	28	31	3	28	28	34	23	34	31	3	2	15		3		2		1	4	7	1	1		
	2	6	4		3	2	2	3	1	3	4		2	7	11	7	5	5	1		1	2	1	2	1		1		
	2	1	2	2		8	3		9	8	9	1		16		2	6												

1998-99

1 Aug	15	(h)	Leicester C	D	2-2	Sheringham, Beckham	55,052
2	22	(a)	West Ham U	D	0-0		25,912
3 Sep	9	(h)	Charlton Ath	W	4-1	Solskjaer 2, Yorke 2	55,147
4	12	(h)	Coventry C	W	2-0	Yorke, Johnsen	55,193
5	20	(a)	Arsenal	L	0-3		38,142
6	24	(h)	Liverpool	W	2-0	Irwin (pen), Scholes	55,181
7 Oct	3	(a)	Southampton	W	3-0	Yorke, Cole, Cruyff	15,251
8	17	(h)	Wimbledon	W	5-1	Cole 2, Giggs, Beckham, Yorke	55,265
9	24	(a)	Derby Co	D	1-1	Cruyff	30,867
10	31	(a)	Everton	W	4-1	Yorke, Short (og), Cole, Blomqvist	40,087
11 Nov	8	(h)	Newcastle U	D	0-0		55,174
12	14	(h)	Blackburn R	W	3-2	Scholes 2, Yorke	55,198
13	21	(a)	Sheffield W	L	1-3	Cole	39,475
14	29	(h)	Leeds U	W	3-2	Solskjaer, Keane, Butt	55,172
15 Dec	5	(a)	Aston Villa	D	1-1	Scholes	39,241
16	12	(a)	Tottenham H	D	2-2	Solskjaer 2	36,058
17	16	(h)	Chelsea	D	1-1	Cole	55,159
18	19	(h)	Middlesbrough	L	2-3	Butt, Scholes	55,152
19	26	(h)	Nottingham F	W	3-0	Johnsen 2, Giggs	55,216
20	29	(a)	Chelsea	D	0-0		34,741
21 Jan	10	(h)	West Ham U	W	4-1	Yorke, Cole 2, Solskjaer	55,180
22	16	(a)	Leicester C	W	6-2	Yorke 3, Cole 2, Stam	22,091
23	31	(a)	Charlton Ath	W	1-0	Yorke	20,043
24 Feb	3	(h)	Derby Co	W	1-0	Yorke	55,174
25	6	(a)	Nottingham F	W	8-1	Yorke 2, Cole 2, Solskjaer 4	30,025
26	17	(h)	Arsenal	D	1-1	Cole	55,171
27	20	(a)	Coventry C	W	1-0	Giggs	22,594
28	27	(h)	Southampton	W	2-1	Keane, Yorke	55,316
29 Mar	13	(a)	Newcastle U	W	2-1	Cole 2	36,776
30	21	(h)	Everton	W	3-1	Solskjaer, G. Neville, Beckham	55,182
31 Apr	3	(a)	Wimbledon	D	1-1	Beckham	26,121
32	17	(h)	Sheffield W	W	3-0	Solskjaer, Sheringham, Scholes	55,270
33	25	(a)	Leeds U	D	1-1	Cole	40,255
34 May	1	(h)	Aston Villa	W	2-1	Watson (og), Beckham	55,189
35	5	(a)	Liverpool	D	2-2	Yorke, Irwin (pen)	44,702
36	9	(a)	Middlesbrough	W	1-0	Yorke	34,655
37	12	(a)	Blackburn R	D	0-0		30,436
38	16	(h)	Tottenham H	W	2-1	Beckham, Cole	55,189

FINAL LEAGUE POSITION: 1st in F.A. Carling Premiership

Appearances

Sub. Appearances

Goals

Schmeichel	Neville G	Irwin	Keane	Johnsen	Stam	Beckham	Butt	Cole	Scholes	Giggs	Sheringham	Berg	Yorke	Neville P	Solskjaer	Blomqvist	Van der Gouw	Brown	Cruyff	Curtis	Greening	May	
1	2*	3	4	5	6†	7	8	9	10	11	12	13											1
1	2†	3	5	6		7	8	9*		11	12	4	10	13									2
1		2*	5	4	6	7		13	11		14	12	10°	3	9†	8							3
1	2		5	4†	6	7*	12		10	11°		13	9	3	8	14							4
1	2	3	5	6		7	8			11		4	9	10									5
1	4	3	5	6		7	12	13	10*	11			9	2	8†								6
	4	3†	5	6	7	8	9				12		11*	2	10°		1	13	14				7
	4		5	6	7†		9	12	11*				10	3°		8	1	2	13	14			8
1	4*		5	6	7	8°	9	12	11†				10	3		14		2	13				9
1	4	12†	5	6		7	9			11			10	3*		8		2					10
1	4	3	5	12†	6	7	13	9		11			10		14	8°		2*					11
1	4	14		6	7	8	9			11†			10	2	12			5*	13°	3			12
1	4	3°	5†	6		7	12	9		11			10	2	13	8*		14					13
1	4		5		6°		8	9*		11†	12	13	14	10	3	7		2					14
1	4	3	5	6		7	12	9*		11		13	10			8†		2					15
1	2		5	4	6	7	8	12	11°		10*	13		3	9†	14							16
1	4	3	5	6		12	8	9	11°		13	14	10*			7†		2					17
1	4	3	5	6	7*	8	9	12		11			10	2†	13								18
1		3	5°	6		7	8	9†	11*		10	4		2	13	12					14		19
1	2	3	5	4	6	7	8	9	10*	11	12												20
		3	5†	12	6	8°	9			11		4	10		14	7	1	2*	13				21
1		3	5	6	7		9			11		4	10		12	8		2*					22
1	2	3	5	6	7†	8*	9	12		11		4	10		13								23
1	2	3	5	4	6		8	7		11*			10	9	12								24
1	2		5†	4	6	7	12	9		11			10°	3	13	8*		14					25
1	2		5*	4	6	7	8	9		13	12		10	3		11†							26
1	2	3	5	4	6*	7		9°	8	11		12	10†	13	14								27
1	2	12	13	6		7	8†	14	5	11		4	10	3*	9°								28
1°	2	3	5	12	6	7	9	8†	11*			4	10	13	14								29
1	2		5	6	7°	8	9*				12	4	10	3	11†				13	14			30
1	2	3	5	6		7	9	8				4	10		12	11*							31
	2	12	5†	6°		8				11			10	3	9	7*	1	4	13	14			32
1	2	3*	5			7†	8	9		13		14	10	12		11°		6		4			33
1	2	3		6		7	8		5				10	9	12	11*		13		4†			34
1	2	3	5	4	6	7	12	9*	8				10	13		11†							35
1	2	3	5*	6		7	12	13	8°				10	9	14	11†				4			36
1	2	3	4	6°		7	8	9†	12	11		13	10	5*	14								37
1	2	3	5	6		7	12	13	8*	11°	10†		9		14					4			38
34	34	26	33	19	30	33	22	26	24	20	7	10	32	19	9	20	4	11	1	4			
		3	2	3		1	9	6	7	4	10	6		9	10	5	1	3	5	3	3	2	
	1	2	2	3	1	6	2	17	6	3	2		18		12	1		2					

1974-75 SEASON

SECOND DIVISION

	P	W	D	L	F	A	Pts
Manchester United	42	26	9	7	66	30	61
Aston Villa	42	25	8	9	69	32	58
Norwich City	42	20	13	9	58	37	53
Sunderland	42	19	13	10	65	35	51
Bristol City	42	21	8	13	47	33	50
West Brom. Albion	42	18	9	15	54	42	45
Blackpool	42	14	17	11	38	33	45
Hull City	42	15	14	13	40	53	44
Fulham	42	13	16	13	44	39	42
Bolton	42	15	12	15	45	41	42
Oxford United	42	15	12	15	41	51	42
Orient	42	11	20	11	28	39	42
Southampton	42	15	11	16	53	54	41
Notts County	42	12	16	14	49	59	40
York City	42	14	10	18	51	55	38
Nottingham Forest	42	12	14	16	43	55	38
Portsmouth	42	12	13	17	44	54	37
Oldham Athletic	42	10	15	17	40	48	35
Bristol Rovers	42	12	11	19	42	64	35
Millwall	42	10	12	20	44	56	32
Cardiff City	42	9	14	19	36	62	32
Sheffield Wednesday	42	5	11	26	29	64	21

1975-76 SEASON

FIRST DIVISION

	P	W	D	L	F	A	Pts
Liverpool	42	23	14	5	66	31	60
Q.P.R.	42	24	11	7	67	33	59
Manchester United	42	23	10	10	68	42	56
Derby County	42	21	11	10	75	58	53
Leeds United	42	21	9	12	65	46	51
Ipswich Town	42	16	14	12	54	48	46
Leicester City	42	13	19	10	48	51	45
Manchester City	42	16	12	15	64	46	43
Tottenham Hotspur	42	14	15	13	63	63	43
Norwich City	42	16	10	16	58	58	42
Everton	42	15	12	15	60	66	42
Stoke City	42	15	11	16	48	50	41
Middlesbrough	42	15	10	17	46	45	40
Coventry City	42	13	14	15	47	57	40
Newcastle United	42	15	9	18	71	62	39
Aston Villa	42	11	17	14	51	59	39
Arsenal	42	13	10	19	47	53	36
West Ham United	42	13	10	19	48	71	36
Birmingham City	42	13	7	22	57	75	33
Wolves	42	10	10	22	51	68	30
Burnley	42	9	10	23	43	66	28
Sheffield United	42	6	10	26	33	82	22

1976-77 SEASON

FIRST DIVISION

	P	W	D	L	F	A	Pts
Liverpool	42	23	11	8	62	33	57
Manchester City	42	21	14	7	60	34	56
Ipswich Town	42	22	8	12	66	39	52
Aston Villa	42	22	7	13	76	50	51
Newcastle United	42	18	13	11	64	49	49
Manchester United	42	18	11	13	71	62	47
West Brom. Albion	42	16	13	13	62	56	45
Arsenal	42	16	11	15	64	59	43
Everton	42	14	14	14	62	64	42
Leeds United	42	15	12	15	48	51	42
Leicester City	42	12	18	12	47	60	42
Middlesbrough	42	14	13	15	40	45	41
Birmingham City	42	13	12	17	63	61	38
Q.P.R.	42	13	12	17	47	52	38
Derby County	42	9	19	14	50	55	37
Norwich City	42	14	9	19	47	64	37
West Ham United	42	11	14	17	46	65	36
Bristol City	42	11	13	18	38	48	35
Coventry City	42	10	15	17	48	59	35
Sunderland	42	11	12	19	46	54	34
Stoke City	42	10	14	18	28	51	34
Tottenham Hotspur	42	12	9	21	48	72	33

1977-78 SEASON

FIRST DIVISION

	P	W	D	L	F	A	Pts
Nottingham Forest	42	25	14	3	69	24	64
Liverpool	42	24	9	9	65	34	57
Everton	42	22	11	9	76	45	55
Manchester City	42	20	12	10	74	51	52
Arsenal	42	21	10	11	60	37	52
West Brom. Albion	42	18	14	10	62	53	50
Coventry City	42	18	12	12	75	62	48
Aston Villa	42	18	10	14	57	42	46
Leeds United	42	18	10	14	63	53	46
Manchester United	42	16	10	16	67	63	42
Birmingham City	42	16	9	17	55	60	41
Derby County	42	14	13	15	54	59	41
Norwich City	42	11	18	13	52	66	40
Middlesbrough	42	12	15	15	42	54	39
Wolves	42	12	12	18	51	64	36
Chelsea	42	11	14	17	46	69	36
Bristol City	42	11	13	18	49	53	35
Ipswich Town	42	11	13	18	47	61	35
Q.P.R.	42	9	15	18	47	64	33
West Ham United	42	12	8	22	52	69	32
Newcastle United	42	6	10	26	42	78	22
Leicester City	42	5	12	25	26	70	22

1978-79 SEASON

FIRST DIVISION

	P	W	D	L	F	A	Pts
Liverpool	42	30	8	4	85	16	68
Nottingham Forest	42	21	18	3	61	26	60
West Brom. Albion	42	24	11	7	72	35	59
Everton	42	17	17	8	52	40	51
Leeds United	42	18	14	10	70	52	50
Ipswich Town	42	20	9	13	63	49	49
Arsenal	42	17	14	11	61	48	48
Aston Villa	42	15	16	11	59	49	46
Manchester United	42	15	15	12	60	63	45
Coventry City	42	14	16	12	58	68	44
Tottenham Hotspur	42	13	15	14	48	61	41
Middlesbrough	42	15	10	17	57	50	40
Bristol City	42	15	10	17	47	51	40
Southampton	42	12	16	14	47	53	40
Manchester City	42	13	13	16	58	56	39
Norwich City	42	7	23	12	51	57	37
Bolton Wanderers	42	12	11	19	54	75	35
Wolves	42	13	8	21	44	68	34
Derby County	42	10	11	21	44	71	31
Q.P.R.	42	6	13	23	45	73	25
Birmingham City	42	6	10	26	37	64	22
Chelsea	42	5	10	27	44	92	20

1979-80 SEASON

FIRST DIVISION

Liverpool	42	25	10	7	81	30	60
Manchester United	42	24	10	8	65	35	58
Ipswich Town	42	22	9	11	68	39	53
Arsenal	42	18	16	8	52	36	52
Nottingham Forest	42	20	8	14	63	43	48
Wolves	42	19	9	14	58	47	47
Aston Villa	42	16	14	12	51	50	46
Southampton	42	18	9	15	65	53	45
Middlesbrough	42	16	12	14	50	44	44
West Brom. Albion	42	11	19	12	54	50	41
Leeds United	42	13	14	15	46	50	40
Norwich City	42	13	14	15	58	66	40
Crystal Palace	42	12	16	14	41	50	40
Tottenham Hotspur	42	15	10	17	52	62	40
Coventry City	42	16	7	19	56	66	39
Brighton & Hove Alb.	42	11	15	16	47	57	37
Manchester City	42	12	13	17	43	66	37
Stoke City	42	13	10	19	44	58	36
Everton	42	9	17	16	43	51	35
Bristol City	42	9	13	20	37	66	31
Derby County	42	11	8	23	47	67	30
Bolton Wanderers	42	5	15	22	38	73	25

1980-81 SEASON

FIRST DIVISION

Aston Villa	42	26	8	8	72	40	60
Ipswich Town	42	23	10	9	77	43	56
Arsenal	42	19	15	8	61	45	53
West Brom. Albion	42	20	12	10	60	42	52
Liverpool	42	17	17	8	62	46	51
Southampton	42	20	10	12	76	56	50
Nottingham Forest	42	19	12	11	62	45	50
Manchester United	42	15	18	9	51	36	48
Leeds United	42	17	10	15	39	47	44
Tottenham Hotspur	42	14	15	13	70	68	43
Stoke City	42	12	18	12	51	60	42
Manchester City	42	14	11	17	56	59	39
Birmingham City	42	13	12	17	50	61	38
Middlesbrough	42	16	5	21	53	51	37
Everton	42	13	10	19	55	58	36
Coventry City	42	13	10	19	48	68	36
Sunderland	42	14	7	21	58	53	35
Wolves	42	13	9	20	47	55	35
Brighton & Hove Alb.	42	14	7	21	54	67	35
Norwich City	42	13	7	22	49	73	33
Leicester City	42	13	6	23	40	67	32
Crystal Palace	42	6	7	29	47	83	19

1981-82 SEASON

FIRST DIVISION

Liverpool	42	26	9	7	80	32	87
Ipswich Town	42	26	5	11	75	53	83
Manchester United	42	22	12	8	59	29	78
Tottenham Hotspur	42	20	11	11	67	48	71
Arsenal	42	20	11	11	48	37	71
Swansea City	42	21	6	15	58	51	69
Southampton	42	19	9	14	72	67	66
Everton	42	17	13	12	56	50	64
West Ham United	42	14	16	12	66	57	58
Manchester City	42	15	13	14	49	50	58
Aston Villa	42	15	12	15	55	53	57
Nottingham Forest	42	15	12	15	42	48	57
Brighton & Hove Alb.	42	13	13	16	43	52	52
Coventry City	42	13	11	18	56	62	50
Notts County	42	13	8	21	45	69	47
Birmingham City	42	10	14	18	53	61	44
West Brom. Albion	42	11	11	20	46	57	44
Stoke City	42	12	8	22	44	63	44
Sunderland	42	11	11	20	38	58	44
Leeds United	42	10	12	20	39	61	42
Wolves	42	10	10	22	32	63	40
Middlesbrough	42	8	15	19	34	52	39

1982-83 SEASON

FIRST DIVISION

Liverpool	42	24	10	8	87	37	82
Watford	42	22	5	15	74	57	71
Manchester United	42	19	13	8	56	38	70
Tottenham Hotspur	42	20	9	13	65	50	69
Nottingham Forest	42	20	9	13	62	50	69
Aston Villa	42	21	5	16	62	50	68
Everton	42	18	10	14	66	48	64
West Ham United	42	20	4	18	68	62	64
Ipswich Town	42	15	13	14	64	50	58
Arsenal	42	16	10	16	58	56	58
West Brom. Albion	42	15	12	15	51	49	57
Southampton	42	15	12	15	54	58	57
Stoke City	42	16	9	17	53	64	57
Norwich City	42	14	12	16	52	58	54
Notts County	42	15	7	21	55	71	52
Sunderland	42	12	14	16	48	61	50
Birmingham City	42	12	15	16	40	55	50
Luton Town	42	12	13	17	65	84	49
Coventry City	42	13	9	20	48	59	48
Manchester City	42	13	8	21	47	70	47
Swansea City	42	10	11	21	51	69	41
Brighton & Hove Alb.	42	9	13	20	38	67	40

1983-84 SEASON

FIRST DIVISION

Liverpool	42	22	14	6	73	32	80
Southampton	42	22	11	9	66	38	77
Nottingham Forest	42	22	8	12	76	45	74
Manchester United	42	20	14	8	71	41	74
Q.P.R.	42	22	7	13	67	37	73
Arsenal	42	18	9	15	74	60	63
Everton	42	16	14	12	44	42	62
Tottenham Hotspur	42	17	10	15	64	65	61
West Ham United	42	17	9	16	60	55	60
Aston Villa	42	17	9	16	59	61	60
Watford	42	16	9	17	68	77	57
Ipswich Town	42	15	8	19	55	57	53
Sunderland	42	13	13	16	42	53	52
Norwich City	42	12	15	15	48	49	51
Leicester City	42	13	12	17	65	68	51
Luton Town	42	14	9	19	53	66	51
West Brom. Albion	42	14	9	19	48	62	51
Stoke City	42	13	11	18	44	63	50
Coventry City	42	13	11	18	57	77	50
Birmingham City	42	12	12	18	39	50	48
Notts County	42	10	11	21	50	72	41
Wolves	42	6	11	25	27	80	29

1984-85 SEASON

FIRST DIVISION

	P	W	D	L	F	A	Pts
Everton	42	28	6	8	88	43	90
Liverpool	42	22	11	9	78	35	77
Tottenham Hotspur	42	23	8	11	78	51	77
Manchester United	42	22	10	10	77	47	76
Southampton	42	19	11	12	56	47	68
Chelsea	42	18	12	12	63	48	66
Arsenal	42	19	9	14	61	49	66
Sheffield Wednesday	42	17	14	11	58	45	65
Nottingham Forest	42	19	7	16	56	48	64
Aston Villa	42	15	11	16	60	60	56
Watford	42	14	13	15	81	71	55
West Brom	42	16	7	19	58	62	55
Luton Town	42	15	9	18	57	61	54
Newcastle United	42	13	13	16	55	70	52
Leicester City	42	15	6	21	65	73	51
West Ham United	42	13	12	17	51	68	51
Ipswich Town	42	13	11	18	46	57	50
Coventry City	42	15	5	22	47	64	50
Q.P.R.	42	13	11	18	53	72	50
Norwich City	42	13	10	19	46	64	49
Sunderland	42	10	10	22	40	62	40
Stoke City	42	3	8	31	24	91	17

1985-86 SEASON

FIRST DIVISION

	P	W	D	L	F	A	Pts
Liverpool	42	26	10	6	89	37	88
Everton	42	26	8	8	87	41	86
West Ham United	42	26	6	10	74	40	84
Manchester United	42	22	10	10	70	36	76
Sheffield Wednesday	42	21	10	11	63	54	73
Chelsea	42	20	11	11	57	56	71
Arsenal	42	20	9	13	49	47	69
Nottingham Forest	42	19	11	12	69	53	68
Luton Town	42	18	12	12	61	44	66
Tottenham Hotspur	42	19	8	15	74	52	65
Newcastle United	42	17	12	13	67	72	63
Watford	42	16	11	15	69	62	59
Q.P.R.	42	15	7	20	53	64	52
Southampton	42	12	10	20	51	62	46
Manchester City	42	11	12	19	43	57	45
Aston Villa	42	10	14	18	51	67	44
Coventry City	42	11	10	21	48	71	43
Oxford United	42	10	12	20	62	80	42
Leicester City	42	10	12	20	54	76	42
Ipswich Town	42	11	8	23	32	55	41
Birmingham City	42	8	5	29	30	73	29
West Brom	42	4	12	26	35	89	24

1986-87 SEASON

FIRST DIVISION

	P	W	D	L	F	A	Pts
Everton	42	26	8	8	76	31	86
Liverpool	42	23	8	11	72	42	77
Tottenham Hotspur	42	21	8	13	68	43	71
Arsenal	42	20	10	12	58	35	70
Norwich City	42	17	17	8	53	51	68
Wimbledon	42	19	9	14	57	50	66
Luton Town	42	18	12	12	47	45	66
Nottingham Forest	42	18	11	13	64	51	65
Watford	42	18	9	15	67	54	63
Coventry City	42	17	12	13	50	45	63
Manchester United	42	14	14	14	52	45	56
Southampton	42	14	10	18	69	68	52
Sheffield Wednesday	42	13	13	16	58	59	52
Chelsea	42	13	13	16	53	64	52
West Ham United	42	14	10	18	52	67	52
Q.P.R.	42	13	11	18	48	64	50
Newcastle United	42	12	11	19	47	65	47
Oxford United	42	11	13	18	44	69	46
Charlton Athletic	42	11	11	20	45	55	44
Leicester City	42	11	9	22	54	76	42
Manchester City	42	8	15	19	36	57	39
Aston Villa	42	8	12	22	45	79	36

1987-88 SEASON

FIRST DIVISION

	P	W	D	L	F	A	Pts
Liverpool	40	26	12	2	87	24	90
Manchester United	40	23	12	5	71	38	81
Nottingham Forest	40	20	13	7	67	39	73
Everton	40	19	13	8	53	27	70
Q.P.R.	40	19	10	11	48	38	67
Arsenal	40	18	12	10	58	39	66
Wimbledon	40	14	15	11	58	47	57
Newcastle United	40	14	14	12	55	53	56
Luton Town	40	14	11	15	57	58	53
Coventry City	40	13	14	13	46	53	53
Sheffield Wednesday	40	15	8	17	52	66	53
Southampton	40	12	14	14	49	53	50
Tottenham Hotspur	40	12	11	17	38	48	47
Norwich City	40	12	9	19	40	52	45
Derby County	40	10	13	17	35	45	43
West Ham United	40	9	15	16	40	52	42
Charlton Athletic	40	9	15	16	38	52	42
Chelsea	40	9	15	16	50	68	42
Portsmouth	40	7	14	19	36	66	35
Watford	40	7	11	22	27	51	32
Oxford United	40	6	13	21	44	80	31

1988-89 SEASON

FIRST DIVISION

	P	W	D	L	F	A	Pts
Arsenal	38	22	10	6	73	36	76
Liverpool	38	22	10	6	65	28	76
Nottingham Forest	38	17	13	8	64	43	64
Norwich City	38	17	11	10	48	45	62
Derby County	38	17	7	14	40	38	58
Tottenham Hotspur	38	15	12	11	60	46	57
Coventry City	38	14	13	11	47	42	55
Everton	38	14	12	12	50	45	54
Q.P.R.	38	14	11	13	43	37	53
Millwall	38	14	11	13	47	52	53
Manchester United	38	13	12	13	45	35	51
Wimbledon	38	14	9	15	50	46	51
Southampton	38	10	15	13	52	66	45
Charlton Athletic	38	10	12	16	44	58	42
Sheffield Wednesday	38	10	12	16	34	51	42
Luton Town	38	10	11	17	42	52	41
Aston Villa	38	9	13	16	45	56	40
Middlesbrough	38	9	12	17	44	61	39
West Ham United	38	10	8	20	37	62	38
Newcastle United	38	7	10	21	32	63	31

1989-90 SEASON

FIRST DIVISION

Liverpool	38	23	10	5	78	37	79
Aston Villa	38	21	7	10	57	38	70
Tottenham Hotspur	38	19	6	13	59	47	63
Arsenal	38	18	8	12	54	38	62
Chelsea	38	16	12	10	58	50	60
Everton	38	17	8	13	51	33	59
Southampton	38	15	10	13	71	63	55
Wimbledon	38	13	16	9	47	40	55
Nottingham Forest	38	15	9	14	55	47	54
Norwich City	38	13	14	11	44	42	53
Q.P.R.	38	13	11	14	45	44	50
Coventry City	38	14	7	17	39	59	49
Manchester United	**38**	**13**	**9**	**16**	**46**	**47**	**48**
Manchester City	38	12	12	14	43	52	48
Crystal Palace	38	13	9	16	42	66	48
Derby County	38	13	7	18	43	40	46
Luton Town	38	10	13	15	43	57	43
Sheffield Wednesday	38	11	10	17	35	51	43
Charlton Athletic	38	7	9	22	31	57	30
Millwall	38	5	11	22	39	65	26

1990-91 SEASON

FIRST DIVISION

Arsenal	38	24	13	1	74	18	83
Liverpool	38	23	7	8	77	40	76
Crystal Palace	38	20	9	9	50	41	69
Leeds United	38	19	7	12	65	47	64
Manchester City	38	17	11	10	64	53	62
Manchester United	**38**	**16**	**12**	**10**	**58**	**45**	**59**
Wimbledon	38	14	14	10	53	46	56
Nottingham Forest	38	14	12	12	65	50	54
Everton	38	13	12	13	50	46	51
Tottenham	38	11	16	11	51	50	49
Chelsea	38	13	10	15	58	69	49
Q.P.R.	38	12	10	16	44	53	46
Sheffield United	38	13	7	18	36	55	46
Southampton	38	12	9	17	58	69	45
Norwich City	38	13	6	19	41	64	45
Coventry City	38	11	11	16	42	49	44
Aston Villa	38	9	14	15	46	58	41
Luton Town	38	10	7	21	42	61	37
Sunderland	38	8	10	20	38	60	34
Derby County	38	5	9	24	37	75	24

Arsenal 2 points deducted
Manchester United 1 point deducted

1991-92 SEASON

FIRST DIVISION

Leeds United	42	22	16	4	74	37	82
Manchester United	**42**	**21**	**15**	**6**	**63**	**33**	**78**
Sheffield Wednesday	42	21	12	9	62	49	75
Arsenal	42	19	15	8	81	46	72
Manchester City	42	20	10	12	61	48	70
Liverpool	42	16	16	10	47	40	64
Aston Villa	42	17	9	16	48	44	60
Nottingham Forest	42	16	11	15	60	58	59
Sheffield United	42	16	9	17	65	63	57
Crystal Palace	42	14	15	13	53	61	57
Q.P.R.	42	12	18	12	48	47	54
Everton	42	13	14	15	52	51	53
Wimbledon	42	13	14	15	53	53	53
Chelsea	42	13	14	15	50	60	53
Tottenham	42	15	7	20	58	63	52
Southampton	42	14	10	18	39	55	52
Oldham Athletic	42	14	9	19	63	67	51
Norwich City	42	11	12	19	47	63	45
Coventry City	42	11	11	20	35	44	44
Luton Town	42	10	12	20	38	71	42
Notts County	42	10	10	22	40	62	40
West Ham United	42	9	11	22	37	59	38

1992-93 SEASON

PREMIER DIVISION

Manchester United	**42**	**24**	**12**	**6**	**67**	**31**	**84**
Aston Villa	42	21	11	10	57	40	74
Norwich City	42	21	9	12	61	65	72
Blackburn Rovers	42	20	11	11	68	46	71
Q.P.R.	42	17	12	13	63	55	63
Liverpool	42	16	11	15	62	55	59
Sheffield Wednesday	42	15	14	13	55	51	59
Tottenham	42	16	11	15	60	66	59
Manchester City	42	15	12	15	56	51	57
Arsenal	42	15	11	16	40	38	56
Chelsea	42	14	14	14	51	54	56
Wimbledon	42	14	12	16	56	55	54
Everton	42	15	8	19	53	55	53
Sheffield United	42	14	10	18	54	53	52
Coventry City	42	13	13	16	52	57	52
Ipswich Town	42	12	16	14	50	55	52
Leeds United	42	12	15	15	57	62	51
Southampton	42	13	11	18	54	61	50
Oldham Athletic	42	13	10	19	63	74	49
Crystal Palace	42	11	16	15	48	61	49
Middlesbrough	42	11	11	20	54	75	44
Nottingham Forest	42	10	10	22	41	62	40

1993-94 SEASON

F.A. PREMIERSHIP

Manchester United	**42**	**27**	**11**	**4**	**80**	**38**	**92**
Blackburn Rovers	42	25	9	8	63	36	84
Newcastle United	42	23	8	11	82	41	77
Arsenal	42	18	17	7	53	28	71
Leeds United	42	18	16	8	65	39	70
Wimbledon	42	18	11	13	56	53	65
Sheffield Wednesday	42	16	16	10	76	54	64
Liverpool	42	17	9	16	59	55	60
Q.P.R.	42	16	12	14	62	64	60
Aston Villa	42	15	12	15	46	50	57
Coventry City	42	14	14	14	43	45	56
Norwich City	42	12	17	13	65	61	53
West Ham United	42	13	13	16	47	58	52
Chelsea	42	13	12	17	49	53	51
Tottenham Hotspur	42	11	12	19	54	59	45
Manchester City	42	9	18	15	38	49	45
Everton	42	12	8	22	42	63	44
Southampton	42	12	7	23	49	66	43
Ipswich Town	42	9	16	17	35	58	43
Sheffield United	42	8	18	16	42	60	42
Oldham Athletic	42	9	13	20	42	68	40
Swindon Town	42	5	15	22	47	100	30

1994-95 SEASON

F.A. PREMIERSHIP

Blackburn Rovers	42	27	8	7	80	39	89
Manchester United	42	26	10	6	77	28	88
Nottingham Forest	42	22	11	9	72	43	77
Liverpool	42	21	11	10	65	37	74
Leeds United	42	20	13	9	59	38	63
Newcastle United	42	20	12	10	67	47	72
Tottenham Hotspur	42	16	14	12	66	58	62
Q.P.R.	42	17	9	16	61	59	60
Wimbledon	42	15	11	16	48	65	56
Southampton	42	12	18	12	61	63	54
Chelsea	42	13	15	14	50	55	54
Arsenal	42	13	12	17	52	49	51
Sheffield Wednesday	42	13	12	17	49	57	51
West Ham United	42	13	11	18	44	48	50
Everton	42	11	17	14	44	51	50
Coventry City	42	12	14	16	44	62	50
Manchester City	42	12	13	17	53	64	49
Aston Villa	42	11	15	16	51	56	48
Crystal Palace	42	11	12	19	34	49	45
Norwich City	42	10	13	19	37	54	43
Leicester City	42	6	11	25	45	80	29
Ipswich Town	42	7	6	29	36	93	27

1995-96 SEASON

F.A. PREMIERSHIP

Manchester United	38	25	7	6	73	35	82
Newcastle United	38	24	6	8	66	37	78
Liverpool	38	20	11	7	70	34	71
Aston Villa	38	18	9	11	52	35	63
Arsenal	38	17	12	9	49	32	63
Everton	38	17	10	11	64	44	61
Blackburn Rovers	38	18	7	13	61	47	61
Tottenham Hotspur	38	16	13	9	50	38	61
Nottingham Forest	38	15	13	10	50	54	58
West Ham United	38	14	9	15	43	52	51
Chelsea	38	12	14	12	46	44	50
Middlesbrough	38	11	10	17	35	50	43
Leeds United	38	12	7	19	40	57	43
Wimbledon	38	10	11	17	55	70	41
Sheffield Wednesday	38	10	10	18	48	61	40
Coventry City	38	8	14	16	42	60	38
Southampton	38	9	11	18	34	52	38
Manchester City	38	9	11	18	33	58	38
Q.P.R.	38	9	6	23	38	57	33
Bolton Wanderers	38	8	5	25	39	71	29

1996-97 SEASON

F.A PREMIERSHIP

Manchester United	38	21	12	5	76	44	75
Newcastle United	38	19	11	8	73	40	68
Arsenal	38	19	11	8	62	32	68
Liverpool	38	19	11	8	62	37	68
Aston Villa	38	17	10	11	47	34	61
Chelsea	38	16	11	11	58	55	59
Sheffield Wednesday	38	14	15	9	50	51	57
Wimbledon	38	15	11	12	49	46	56
Leicester City	38	12	11	15	46	54	47
Tottenham Hotspur	38	13	7	18	44	51	46
Leeds United	38	11	13	14	28	38	46
Derby County	38	11	13	14	45	58	46
Blackburn Rovers	38	9	15	14	42	43	42
West Ham United	38	10	12	16	39	48	42
Everton	38	10	12	16	44	57	42
Southampton	38	10	11	17	50	56	41
Coventry City	38	9	14	15	38	54	41
Sunderland	38	10	10	18	35	53	40
Middlesbrough	38	10	12	16	51	60	39
Nottingham Forest	38	6	16	16	31	59	34

1997-98 SEASON

F.A. PREMIERSHIP

Arsenal	38	23	9	6	68	33	78
Manchester United	38	23	8	7	73	26	77
Liverpool	38	18	11	9	68	42	65
Chelsea	38	20	3	15	71	43	63
Leeds United	38	17	8	13	57	46	59
Blackburn Rovers	38	16	10	12	57	52	58
Aston Villa	38	17	6	15	49	48	57
West Ham United	38	16	8	14	56	57	56
Derby County	38	16	7	15	52	49	55
Leicester City	38	13	14	11	51	41	53
Coventry City	38	12	16	10	46	44	52
Southampton	38	14	6	18	50	55	48
Newcastle United	38	11	11	16	35	44	44
Tottenham Hotspur	38	11	11	16	44	56	44
Wimbledon	38	10	14	14	34	46	44
Sheffield Wednesday	38	12	8	18	52	67	44
Everton	38	9	13	16	41	56	40
Bolton Wanderers	38	9	13	16	41	61	40
Barnsley	38	10	5	23	37	82	35
Crystal Palace	38	8	9	21	37	71	33

1998-99 SEASON

F.A. PREMIERSHIP

Manchester United	38	22	13	3	80	37	79
Arsenal	38	22	12	4	59	17	78
Chelsea	38	20	15	3	57	30	75
Leeds United	38	18	13	7	62	34	67
West Ham United	38	16	9	13	46	53	57
Aston Villa	38	15	10	13	51	46	55
Liverpool	38	15	9	14	68	49	54
Derby County	38	13	13	12	40	45	52
Middlesbrough	38	12	15	11	48	54	51
Leicester City	38	12	13	13	40	46	49
Tottenham Hotspur	38	11	14	13	47	50	47
Sheffield Wednesday	38	13	7	18	41	42	46
Newcastle United	38	11	13	14	48	54	46
Everton	38	11	10	17	42	47	43
Coventry City	38	11	9	18	39	51	42
Wimbledon	38	10	12	16	40	63	42
Southampton	38	11	8	19	37	64	41
Charlton Athletic	38	8	12	18	41	56	36
Blackburn Rovers	38	7	14	17	38	52	35
Nottingham Forest	38	7	9	22	35	69	30